fabulous fizz

fabulous fizz

choosing Champagne and sparkling wine for every occasion

alice king

photography by peter cassidy

RYLAND
PETERS
& SMALL

LONDON NEW YORK

For my Father, who taught me to love
Champagne and Debbie, who drinks almost
as much Champagne as I do!

Senior Designer Louise Leffler
Editors Jane Hughes, Maddalena Bastianelli
Picture and Location Researcher Kate Brunt
Production Patricia Harrington
Head of Design Gabriella Le Grazie
Publishing Director Anne Ryland
Stylist Helen Trent
Food Stylist Bridget Sargeson
Photographer's Assistant Christian Barnett
Indexer Hilary Bird

First published in the United Kingdom in 1999
by Ryland Peters & Small
20–21 Jockey's Fields
London WC1R 4BW
www.rylandpeters.com

This paperback edition first published in 2006

10 9 8 7 6 5 4 3 2 1

The publishers are grateful to A.P. Watt Ltd on behalf of Crystal Hale
& Jocelyn Herbert for permission to quote the extract by H.P. Herbert
on page 93.

Printed in China

ISBN-10: 1 84597 288 0
ISBN-13: 978 1 84597 288 2

A CIP record for this book is available from the British Library

Notes All spoon measurements are level unless specified otherwise.
Ovens should be preheated to the specified temperature. If using a
fan-assisted oven, cooking times should be reduced according to the
manufacturer's instructions.

contents

6 preface

8 introduction

14 the nature of fizz
16 behind the scenes
18 adding the sparkle
22 fizz regions

28 how to choose fizz
30 anytime, anywhere – medium-bodied fizz
54 the ultimate aperitif – aperitif-style fizz
68 fizz with attitude – full-bodied fizz
80 heady stuff – vintage fizz
96 demi-sec bubblies – sweet fizz
104 wicked and red – sparkling reds

106 fizz cocktails and recipes
108 cocktails
116 cooking with fizz

126 enjoying fizz
128 serving fizz
132 gadgets
134 glasses
138 bottle sizes

140 index

144 acknowledgements

This book is a celebration.
A celebration of a long love affair.
If you love life with a passion, you will love Champagne.

preface

this book is a celebration. A celebration of a long love affair. If you love life with a passion, you will love Champagne and other sparkling wines, as do I and all my best friends.

Fizz – as these wines are affectionately called – is the celebration drink. There is simply nothing that can compete with all those dancing bubbles and that wonderfully refreshing and seductive flavour. It is the froth of daydreams – the magic of its taste is a dream come true.

This bubbly affair of mine has been going on for some time. At age 18, I started what was for me the dream job – working as a guide in the cellars at Champagne Heidsieck Monopole, in the city of Reims. I learnt lots of French and a lot more about the making, tasting and, of course, the drinking of Champagne. I was seduced.

One very special Champagne celebration took place when my dream of having a baby at home came true with the birth of my third son, Felix. Within ten minutes of his arrival I drank a glass of Krug Grande Cuvée to celebrate and it was one of the most magical and memorable moments in my life.

So I make no apologies for the fact that a great percentage of this book concentrates on Champagne. For *Fabulous Fizz* is not a comprehensive guide to sparkling wine, more a personal view of some of the greatest fizzes in the world. And that includes some top-class sparklers made in countries as diverse as North America, Australia, Spain and Italy.

But if I had to choose just one wine for my desert island? It would have to be that all-time favourite fabulous fizz made in the north of France – Champagne.

Alice King, June 2006

introduction

Celebratory, stylish and frothy, fizz has been associated with fun for a long time – since the middle of the 17th century when London society first discovered the 'uplifting' effect of this effervescing wine from Champagne. The Champagne region of France is the home of fizz; but sparkling wine is made in many other corners of the world too – the Spanish enjoy bone-dry cava, the Italians love their gently sweet Asti and the New World fizz regions – California, Australia, New Zealand and South Africa – all make amazingly good fizz too.

Just mention fizz and people's eyes will sparkle in anticipation. It's a fabulous tasting drink, with that wonderful bubbly sensation on the tongue. Fizz comes in many guises. It might be pale golden in colour, elegant and restrained in style, with hints of yeasty flavours. Or perhaps it's pale onion-pink, with heady aromas of strawberries; or maybe your ideal fizz is upfront and positively fruity. One of the many joys of sparkling wine is its wealth of styles – no matter what your taste buds prefer, there's a fizz for you. In this book, you'll discover non-vintage, vintage, dry fizzes and sweet fizzes, pink and even red fizzes. And, whatever the occasion, the celebratory style of this frothing wine means you can guarantee that it will be more than welcome.

My aim with this book is to pass on my enthusiasm for fabulous fizz. I have divided my favourite fizzes into three main sections – light aperitif-style, 'anytime, anywhere' medium-bodied fizzes and then the richer styles that often show at their best with food. If you already have some firm fizz favourites, look them up in the index to see which section they fall into. Then you can go out and discover a whole host of other Champagnes and sparkling wines of a similar style. But don't stop there; go on and experiment with others too. There's a whole world of fabulous fizz to suit all palates, pockets and occasions. If you aren't already a fizz fan, I guarantee you soon will be!

For instance, if you want an aperitif to mark the beginning of a special evening, try Champagne Pol Roger White Foil NV. This is a delicious fizz, with exotic hints of ginger and cream aromas and perfect balance. If you are having a laid-back barbecue then you need an 'anytime, anywhere' kind of fizz to see you through, such as Seaview Brut Rosé NV or the fabulous Green Point, both from Australia. I am sure there will be those of you who, like me, will have no difficulty in enjoying more than a few glasses of the richer style of bubblies. The fabulously rich and creamy Krug Grande Cuvée NV takes pride of place in my roll call of 'big' fizzes, while

HERE'S TO CHAMPAGNE, THE DRINK DIVINE THAT MAKES US FORGET OUR TROUBLES; IT'S MADE OF A DOLLAR'S WORTH OF WINE AND THREE DOLLARS' WORTH OF BUBBLES.

Anon.

California produces some fabulous rich fizzes that make great food partners, such as the buttery Korbel Chardonnay NV.

But when it comes to that big romance, or those very special, once-in-a-lifetime celebrations, then perhaps vintage fizz is the answer. The wedding toast, for example, demands a fabulous fizz. You can do no better than the aptly named Iron Horse Wedding Cuvée 1996.

Fizz simply makes a party. The most fabulous party I have ever been to was, without doubt, the Champagne Piper Heidsieck bicentenary celebration in the mid-1980s. Held in the Orangerie and gardens at the Palace of Versailles just outside Paris, it was the most extravagant event that I have ever been to, with 1600 guests invited for the launch of Piper Heidsieck's new deluxe cuvée, Champagne Rare. Entering the gardens as the sun set behind the lake, I watched the fountains magically light up while an orchestra began playing Handel's *Water Music*. White-jacketed waiters were everywhere, each carrying magnums of Champagne. Alongside the Piper Heidsieck Rare 1976, which although ten years old, was still youthful and crisp yet steely, with a wonderfully complex flavour, we were also offered magnums of Piper Heidsieck NV.

Even now, just one taste of Piper Heidsieck reminds me of the splendour of that evening, the long line of crisp, white linen-covered tables spread with silver platters of food on either side of the Orangerie. There was every delicacy you could imagine, from roasted quails and quails' eggs to caviar, lobster, crab, huge langoustines and sizzling stir-fried duck. That was a truly magical evening, ending with a sensational firework display around the Lake of Versailles, and celebrated with very special Champagnes.

But as my own party after the week of tasting bubbly contenders for *Fabulous Fizz* proved, there are plenty of fizzes for the not-so-grand and impromptu occasions too! The bottles of fizz that I'd kept sparkling with trusty chrome Champagne stoppers (see page 133) were stacked on ice in barrels all over the candle-lit garden and in both baths inside the house. The Wurlitzer jukebox played from dusk until dawn, and we dined on Chinese take-away cooked by Damien who runs the local Chinese take-away van. We discovered some great fizzes and some delicious combinations to drink with the Singapore noodles, vegetables with black bean sauce, chicken with water chestnuts and beansprouts, and beef with ginger and garlic. It was the best party I have ever held, and I put it all down to the fabulous fizz!

The inevitable result of tasting all these fizzes was not a hangover, but an excess of Champagne corks. As it was Christmas time, I simply used them as tree decorations, spraying them silver and hanging them on the tree by their wires. It looked very pretty and made everyone smile. There are no doubt 101 other uses for a popped Champagne cork, but one of my favourites is to make a memento for a godchild. Keep one of the corks from the fizz served at the christening party, cut a hole in its base and insert a silver coin. I also have a friend who keeps the corks from the first bottle of fizz she shares with her lovers. I choose not to count them!

Even the bottle itself, particularly a magnum of Champagne, can add to the sense of occasion. Yielding to one of those impulsive desires recently, I opened a bottle of Veuve Clicquot La Grande Dame 1990 to share with a friend who is very label-conscious. Even before tasting it, he remarked that this must be a very classy fizz, because of its stylish, old-fashioned shape and its seal. He was right, this is immensely elegant Champagne! At the other extreme are designer bottles like the minimalist 'J', from California producer Jordan, with its very eye-catching green and yellow 'J' logo. It's a very fine fizz too, with creamy, toasty, biscuity aromas and flavours.

Sparkling wine also makes for both eye-catching and really tasty cocktails (see pages 108–115). The simplest of all and a great choice to order at a restaurant, bar or club is a Kir Royale, refreshing, fruity with a hint of blackcurrant and very stylish, too.

If there's one thing that beats a glass of fizz, it's enjoying fizz with food. And I don't just mean at a dinner party, it can just as easily be brunch, a barbecue, an early supper with your work-mates; any meal can be turned into a special occasion with a glass of sparkling wine. The richer styles of fizz – the vintage sparklers, prestige

cuvées and the full-bodied rosés in particular – really come into their own served with food. They have the weight, the structure and the sheer complexity of character to complement even the richest of creamy sauces and the strongest of spicy flavours.

The most obvious occasion at which fizz is the star, is a party or reception, where hopefully the trays of canapés will come your way more than once. Those more-ish nibbles can range from salty nuts and garlicky olives through to mozzarella and tomato tartlets. What you need is a refreshing, crisp and fruity fizz to partner all those flavours. Try an elegant aperitif-style bubbly, or an affordable, easy-drinking 'anytime' sparkler.

If you really want to impress your guests, serve them a richer style of fizz as an aperitif –- it will whet their appetite too – and continue to pour it with the first course. How about serving Wild Mushroom and Champagne Risotto (see page 118)? Those bold, earthy, creamy flavours will really be enhanced by a rich, biscuity Champagne. Or try a rich fizz with creamy asparagus soup. For a truly fabulous meal, serve sparkling wine throughout.

Fizz is just perfect with fish, particularly with the richer, meatier fish such as sea bass, turbot or monkfish. One of my favourite suppers is a glass or two of fizz with roasted cod steaks in a spicy tomato sauce. As for fizz and seafood, such as lobster and fresh crab, it's a match made in heaven as far as I'm concerned.

It surprised me too the first time I tried it, but fizz with red meat is actually extremely good. In fact there's a whole host of dishes you can enjoy with sparkling wine – anything from spicy Indian dishes to Thai noodles, and scallops with ginger to char-grilled chicken wings with garlic. When it comes to pudding, a demi-sec bubbly can transform even something as simple as home-made fruit ice cream or sorbet served with tiny almond biscuits into a sublime experience. I think the extra prickle of the bubble on the tongue and the citrus-like acidity mean that demi-sec fizzes really can cut through the richness of puddings.

As you'll discover in this book, there are lots of wonderful combinations to experiment with and some delicious recipes to try out. So why choose anything other than fabulous fizz?

ou have to choose six guests, living or dead, whom you would
ny list would be the 17th-century French monk, Dom Pérignon.

behind the scenes

Champagne has been around for centuries, but only since the close of the 1600s has it been intentionally fizzy. Before then it was a fairly thin, acidic still wine that would sometimes irritatingly decide to start fermenting again in the bottle, causing more than a few explosions. Then, in the mid 1700s, the fashionable café society in London took a fancy to the fizzy version; one thing led to another, and it was discovered that adding a judicial spoonful of sugar would cause a second fermentation and result in those magical bubbles on demand. By the turn of the 18th century, Champagne sparkled.

Have you ever played that game where you have to decide on six guests, living or dead, whom you would like to invite to dinner? Whom would you invite? Top of my list would be Dom Pérignon, a French monk who played a key role in creating what has become my favourite drink. Mind you, it would be quite a costly dinner, as I'd have to serve him Moët & Chandon's vintage prestige cuvée, Dom Pérignon, a truly fabulous fizz!

Appointed treasurer at the Abbey of Hautvilliers just outside Epernay in Champagne in 1668, the blessed monk's duties included winemaking. For a long time he was believed to have been the one who 'invented' sparkling Champagne. Although that particular claim to fame is no longer attributed to him, Dom Pérignon introduced some incredibly innovative winemaking techniques, including the art of blending wines from different vineyards to get the best results, and making a white wine out of black grapes. Both these processes remain central to the way fizz is made today.

Another great figure in Champagne's history is the formidable Nicole-Barbe Clicquot-Ponsardin. Widowed while still in her 20s, she took over the running of her husband's business in 1805 and created what has become one of the most famous Champagne houses, Veuve Clicquot Ponsardin. Besides the fact that she was a very successful business woman in a man's world 200 years ago, the 'Grande Dame' claimed immortality through the development of the extraordinary *remuage* process (see page 19).

Throughout the 1800s, as demand for this fabulous fizz spread across Europe, new houses were set up with names such as Bollinger, Louis Roederer, Perrier-Jouët. The methods by which Champagne is now produced were developed and perfected. Champagne became the celebrated drink of the aristocracy. It was drunk at all fashionable Parisian parties, at the Regency Court at Versailles, it was shipped to the Czar in Russia, and demanded by the elite of London society.

And as the 21st century opens, this celebratory drink continues to hold sway. What has changed is the variety of sparkling wines on offer – not only Champagne from France, but cava from spain, Asti from Italy and of course those fabulous fizzes from North America, Australia and New Zealand. I find it incredible to think that it is only in the past ten years or so that 'New World' sparkling wines have really become international stars. In such a short time, producers have taken some breathtaking leaps to catch up with the 300 years of experience enjoyed by the Champenois. Which gives us all a wealth of fabulous fizzes from which to choose...

adding the sparkle

The yeast eats up the sugar and burps out tiny bubbles of carbon dioxide

The majority of fabulous fizzes, be they Champagnes or sparkling wines from around the world, are made using the *méthode champenoise* (called *méthode traditionelle* or, more simply, 'bottle-fermented' outside Champagne). This involves a fascinating, lengthy and tricky process and is one of the reasons why good fizz will never be cheap.

the champagne way

At first fizz is made like any still wine. The grapes are picked, pressed, and fermented, usually in stainless-steel vats although some producers use oak. The resulting wine is still and in colder regions such as Champagne, it tends to be quite acidic and pale. This is where the magic begins. First comes the blending, an art form in itself that ensures the quality and 'house style' of the fizz is consistent. The winemaker tastes wines from the vats of separately fermented juices from individual vineyards and areas and decides on the exact proportions, or *assemblage,* of each that will go into the final blend. The blended wine is then bottled and given a dose of yeast and sugar, which causes the crucial second fermentation. The most imaginative explanation I've been given of what happens during this fermentation is that the yeast eats up the sugar and in effect burps out tiny bubbles of carbon dioxide which remain trapped in the wine, creating a fabulously frothing fizz.

Depending on the quality and style of fizz, the wine will now be left 'on its yeast lees' for anything from a few weeks to several months to allow those yeasty, biscuity, rich aromas and flavours that we associate with fabulous fizz to develop. Then comes the tricky bit. How to remove those tiny dead yeast cells from the wine (leaving it clear) without losing the streams of bubbles? This is where the second magician, the *remueur*, or riddler, as we'd call him in English, appears. The bottles are placed horizontally, neck first, in hinged wooden racks that are kept in the coolest, darkest part of the cellars. Once a day for about two months, each bottle is twisted and tipped up slightly, a process that is known as *remuage*. This gentle disturbance loosens the yeast sediment and it gradually slips into the neck of the bottle, which by the end of the two months, is virtually upside-down in the rack. Amazingly skilled riddlers can turn up to 40,000 bottles a day! The *remuage* is now mainly done by large computer-operated cages called *gyropalettes*, although most prestige cuvées made in Champagne are still riddled by hand.

The necks of the bottles are then gently lowered into a freezing solution causing an ice plug to form around the yeast sediment. If you are lucky enough to be visiting a sparkling wine cellar while this is happening, it's great drama to watch the *dégorgement*, as the cork is removed and the ice plug shoots spectacularly out of the bottle. Inevitably, a little fizz is lost too, so the bottle is quickly topped up with the *dosage*, a quantity of older wine and a small amount of sugar. Even the brut, or dry fizzes are given a small dose of sugar, which is added to balance the acidity that keeps the fizz fresh as it matures.

Finally the fizz is sealed with the famous Champagne cork and wire. The wire muzzle prevents the cork from popping out since the pressure within the bottle is quite something (at least comparable to the pressure in a large truck tyre). Good quality fizzes are then kept in the cellar for at least six months or so before being released.

alternative methods

There are other ways of adding bubbles to sparkling wine. The most successful of these is the *cuve close* or 'tank method', where the second fermentation takes place in a large, sealed tank. As the amount of wine in contact with the yeast is considerably less, these wines tend to lack the complexity of flavour of bottle-fermented fizzes. The quickest, simplest and most crude method of making sparkling wine, and the one used to make some of the cheapest fizzes, is simply to pump carbon dioxide through the wine (the way fizzy soft drinks are made). It is relatively easy to detect a carbonated sparkling wine as the bubbles tend to be much bigger and the wine loses its fizz extremely quickly.

making it pink

To make pink fizz, you have two choices: traditionally, the skins of black grapes are left with the juice after pressing and this 'dyes' the juice, or else red wine is added to the juice until it is sufficiently pink. Rosés come in all shades of pink from pale onion-skin pink to a deep reddish pink.

which remain trapped in the wine, creating that fabulously frothing fizz...

fizz grapes, terms and styles

grapes

Most fabulous fizzes, be they white or rosé, are made from a blend of Pinot Noir and Chardonnay grape. The third 'classic Champagne grape' is Pinot Meunier. But that's not the whole story. As you'll discover in this book, there are stunning Champagnes and sparkling wines made from just Chardonnay, or from a blend of the two Pinots, not to mention blends of other grapes. And there's also some fabulous sparkling wine made from grape varieties such as Muscat and Shiraz (see fizz regions, pages 22–27).

chardonnay

The importance of this white grape when it comes to sparkling wine is that it brings elegance to the fizz; it's the subtle balance of complexity and refined fruit flavour that make Chardonnay such a star performer. It is also believed to have the greatest potential for ageing of the three grapes. A young Chardonnay wine is light and flowery and has a fresh, citrus-like vibrant edge with good acidity; with several years' bottle age it becomes fatter, developing richer, buttery, creamy flavours.

pinot noir

The winsome Pinot Noir adds weight and body – the 'backbone', if you like – and finesse to the blend. And, as an enticing extra, it brings the delicious mouth-watering flavours of strawberries and raspberries. Fizzes made with Pinot Noir sometimes have an attractive, very slight pale-pink tinge from the brief contact of the juice with the black skins during pressing.

pinot meunier

Don't underestimate Pinot Meunier; this black grape is an essential addition to the blend in Champagne, particularly for the non-vintage fizzes. It is wonderfully fruity, rather like a boiled sweet, with a hint of spice, and it brings an easy-drinking style to the wine. Outside the Champagne region, this is the variety that tends to be dropped from the team.

terms and styles

There are certain terms on fizz labels that can give you a clue as to the style or flavour of the dancing bubbles inside. These are some of the most widely used:

méthode champenoise/
bottle-fermented

The all-important clue as to how those bubbles got in the bottle. This is the method used in Champagne, meaning that the second fermentation takes place in the bottle (see page 19). Look for the terms *méthode traditionelle*, 'traditional method', or 'bottle-fermented', on fizzes made outside Champagne.

non-vintage (NV)

One of my favourite styles of fizz. Non-vintage fizzes are made from a blend of wines from several years to achieve a consistency of 'house style' and quality. This means that once you find a non-vintage fizz to your liking, you should be able to buy it any time, anywhere, safe in the knowledge that it will always be as you expect. With several years' bottle age (if you can resist drinking them), these bubblies become softer, richer and more creamy.

vintage

A wine from a single year. The best producers reserve the finest fruit for vintage fizz, which is one good reason why it's so desirable. A vintage sparkler will reflect as much of the character of the vintage as it does of the producer, and so may taste quite different from one year to the next. For example, a fizz made in a very hot year will taste much richer, rounder and less acidic than a fizz produced in a cooler year. In colder, wetter regions such as Champagne, the top vintage fizzes are only made in years when the quality of the grapes is considered special enough. Happily, more often than not. Most good Champagne houses will age their vintage Champagnes for five to seven years before release.

blanc de blancs

Literally translated this means 'white of white', which tells you that the fizz is made using only the Chardonnay grape. When young, these wines can be relatively light, delicate and creamy; with a little more age, *blanc de blancs* fizzes often develop a fabulously rich, toasted, biscuity flavour.

blanc de noirs

Although 'white of black' may sound like a contradiction in terms, it's not. What it tells you is that the fizz has been made using only black grapes – Pinot Noir and Pinot Meunier. And no, you don't have to be a magician to do this. Just cut a black grape in half – it is only the skin that is black, not the pulp. So as long as you take the juice away from the skins quickly after pressing, a white wine can be made using black grapes. A fizz made from black grapes only is always full-bodied and rich.

prestige cuvées/deluxe cuvées

These are the top-of-the-line blends (i.e. cuvées), the really fabulous fizzes with style and quality, to be savoured on special occasions, high days and holidays. Both vintage and non-vintage, prestige cuvées are luxury Champagnes. They taste truly sublime and you can expect to pay for the privilege.

brut (brut réserve)

This is the style of fizz you'll find most often. Very popular, very drinkable, and usually non-vintage, these are 'dry' fizzes, although they do in fact have a touch of balancing sugar in them, which helps makes them so palatable and delicious. (A style not often seen is brut zéro/ultra brut. This is tartly bone-dry as it has had no sugar added with the *dosage* (see page 19). I find this style of fizz tastes rather sour and metallic.)

demi-sec

Just to confuse you, although the translation of *demi-sec* is 'half dry', the best way to describe these delectable fizzes is 'half sweet', because that's just what they are – a wonderful balance of honeyed sweetness and refreshing acidity.

crémant

When you see the word 'crémant' on a bottle label, for example Crémant d'Alsace and Crémant de Loire, it tells you this is a soft, creamy sparkling wine, less fizzy than Champagne. A wine that is gently bubbly rather than furiously fizzy – an example would be the Italian sparkler Asti Spumante – may be described as *pétillant*, or as having a light 'spritz'.

This is a quick tour to introduce you to some of the finest sparkling wine regions in the world, the sources of the fabulous fizzes included in this book. They include the famous, the up-and-coming and the lesser-known places where I've discovered some real gems. If you get the chance to visit, you'll find a number of producers are geared up for visitors and will give you a warm welcome and often a refreshing glass of their fabulous fizz.

france: champagne

Just what is it about this corner of northern France that makes its wines so fabulous? There are those who say the secret lies in the soil, that it is the underlying chalk that imparts such a special character to the grapes. Then there are the grapes themselves, the three classic varieties from which Champagne is made (no others are permitted): Chardonnay, Pinot Noir and Pinot Meunier (see page 20). Then, of course, there is the climate to consider. It's relatively cold and certainly wet. But this is to the advantage of Champagne: the less sun, the more acidity, and vines that have to struggle for some reason will produce delicate fruit with pure yet intense flavours. This is exactly what's needed to create fabulous fizz. And I'd better not forget the human touch, especially the crucial skills of the blender!

fizz regions

It's really a combination of all these factors, plus the carefully upheld traditions and a sprinkling of magic that makes Champagne, for me, still far and away the greatest fizz in the world. The French are very possessive about their unique sparkling heritage. The very name 'Champagne' is almost sanctified – no one outside the region may use it on any product or for any purpose.

The Comité Interprofessionel des Vins de Champagne (CIVC), the governing body that looks after the Champagne industry, is quite prepared to take companies to court to protect the name. The fashion house of Yves St Laurent for one was forced to withdraw a perfume it had named 'Champagne' (did the CIVC really think we'd mistake the two, or be tempted to drink the perfume?!).

The names that roll off the tongue and are most familiar to us, such as Moët & Chandon, Taittinger and Louis Roederer, are the big houses, many of which you can visit. It makes a really special weekend trip, especially in the autumn when the vines have turned the hillsides golden-brown. If you stay in Epernay, in the heart of the vineyards, you can walk from one house to the next, enjoying a glass or two of fizz and exploring the underground cellars. These are an impressive sight: miles and miles of cold, slightly damp tunnels – even a cavernous room at Champagne Mercier that is used for grand banquets – that were dug out of the chalk centuries ago in Gallo-Roman times, and are now filled with bottles of fizz. My idea of heaven.

loire valley

The Loire Valley has a long tradition of sparkling wine production. Indeed Saumur producers claim to have been in the fizz business long before the Champenois. The two styles of fizz to look out for here are sparkling Saumur and Vouvray. Made predominantly from the main grape of the Loire, Chenin Blanc, these are gently sparkling wines with an unusual, soft, elderflower flavour that becomes distinctly more earthy and honeyed as the wine ages. The best sparkling Saumurs and Vouvrays are refreshingly crisp, ideal for summertime parties. Since the appellation was created in 1976, the quality of these wines has improved as small growers now make the fizz with care.

alsace

Compared to the fizzes of the Loire and Champagne, Crémant d'Alsace is a very recent creation. Bottle-fermented fizz was introduced by one of the region's top producers, Dopff 'au Moulin'. The main grape variety is Pinot Blanc, and some Chardonnay makes an appearance. The few good Crémants d'Alsace I've found have a nutty flavour and crisp style.

Miles and miles of cold, slightly damp tunnels, filled with bottles of Champagne – my idea of heaven.

limoux

Blanquette de Limoux is a little-known, fizzy gem that I've discovered, tucked away in the hinterland of the Languedoc region, in the south of France. Made from the aromatic Mauzac grape, the best Blanquettes have wonderful honeyed, spicy aromas and flavours with an attractive earthy character. These distinctive fizzes are technically 'brut', or dry, yet the perfumed nature of the grape gives an attractive impression of sweetness on the palate.

spain

Spain's fabulous fizz is known as cava, and is unbelievably good value for money. Most of it is made in the Penedés region of Catalonia, traditionally using three grape varieties, Macabeo, Parellada and Xarel-lo. As with the grapes used in Champagne, each is considered to bring a particular characteristic to the wine. That said, Chardonnay is playing an increasingly dominant role, so when you see a 'blanc de blancs' cava, this tells you it's made from Chardonnay. Cava has a very distinctive flavour. It's much softer than Champagne, with less perceivable acidity, and a lightly floral, sometimes smoky flavour.

italy

The classic Italian sparklers, Asti Spumante and Moscato d'Asti, come from Piedmont in northern Italy, and are named after the local hilltop town of Asti. They are both made from the Muscat (*Moscato* in Italian) grape, which, though it sounds strange, is best described as 'grapey'! These are wonderfully easy-drinking, softly sparkling fizzes, lower in alcohol (around 7%), very attractively perfumed, and with deliciously fresh, green grape flavours. They are also gently sweet, yet with that thirst-quenching tang of citrussy acidity on the finish. Of the two, Moscato d'Asti is the finer fizz and more consistent in quality.

united kingdom

Ten years ago, I would never have dreamt that English wines could in any way be described as 'fabulous'. Such is the leap forward in winemaking and planting of better quality grapes, including Chardonnay, that there are now several quite stunning sparkling wines. It makes sense, after all, we have a 'cool' climate and there are chalky soils across south-eastern England, just as there are in Champagne...

north america

As a novice journalist, aged 21, I was sent by UK wine magazine *Decanter* to interview a reader at his rather grand home. I was offered a glass of fizz, which I very happily accepted. It was rich and creamy with the most wonderfully more-ish raspberry and cream overtones. Having spent a spell working in the Champagne region, I thought I knew a thing or two about fizz, and presumed we were drinking some

serious vintage Champagne. Wrong! I was amazed to learn we were drinking Californian fizz, a sensationally complex Schramsberg Blanc de Noirs from one of California's top sparkling wine producers. It was in fact Schramsberg who began the whole sparkling wine trend in the States back in 1965, concentrating on making fizz from Chardonnay, Pinot Noir and Pinot Blanc. These fizzes swiftly became the models that all others aspired to equal.

California now heads the list of sparkling wine states in the USA, closely shadowed in terms of quality if not quantity by her Pacific Northwest neighbours – witness the excellent Argyle from Oregon and the fizzes from Château Ste-Michelle in Washington State – with New York State representing the East Coast. Chardonnay and Pinot Noir have been planted in the best sites to get that all-important tangy acidity and finesse of character. Carneros, Sonoma and Mendocino Counties are now home to some of the most well known and fabulous of California's fizzes, wines that positively burst with mouth-watering, upfront fruit. The Champenois were also quick to jump on the fizz bandwagon. Today, companies including Moët & Chandon (Domaine Chandon), Mumm, and Taittinger (Domaine Carneros) all have major sparkling wine interests in California. So too do the cava producers Freixenet (Gloria Ferrer) and Codorníu.

australia

Australia is a must for any fan of fabulous fizz. Rather like the still wines from this huge and prolific grape-growing continent, Australia's sparkling wines offer huge diversity. It gets a big thumbs-up from me for the very affordable, easy-drinking, everyday party bubblies, not to mention the stunningly classy rich fizzes that are grand enough for the smartest occasions. As for the unique sparkling reds, mostly made from the spicy, fruity Shiraz grape, these have to be tasted to be believed.

While Australia can trace its sparkling wine history back over 100 years, its current thriving industry really kicked in around the same time as California when the world woke up to this fabulous drink and wanted more of these refreshing bubblies. The astute Aussie winemakers sought out the coolest areas, such as Great Western, in Victoria, and planted the classic Champagne grapes. The top sparklers are mostly Chardonnay/Pinot Noir blends, while the easy-drinking, fruity fizzes for those 'anytime' moments can be blends of a number of grape varieties.

Again, the Champenois spotted a good thing and in the 1980s Moët & Chandon flew in and set up Domaine Chandon at Green Point, in the Yarra Valley, Victoria. Green Point, along with the Aussie Seaview and Seppelt fizzes, represent fantastic value for money in the middle price bracket.

A relative newcomer to the fizz stakes, once started it seems there's no stopping New Zealand. The fizzes are crisp, and dry with wonderful finesse and style.

new zealand

A relative newcomer to the fizz stakes, once started it seems there's no stopping New Zealand. The bubblies are currently going from strength to strength, exhibiting depths of flavour that even ten years ago would have been unthinkable. All good news for fizz lovers! In terms of style and taste, the biggest compliment I can pay New Zealand fizz is that I can be hard put to differentiate between top New Zealand fizz and the best of Champagne. New Zealand fizzes are crisp and dry, with a wonderful finesse and style. The leading producers are based on the South Island, in the cool – and inevitably wet – Marlborough region, where, fortunately for us, the somewhat bland and widely planted Müller-Thurgau grape was ignored in favour of Chardonnay and Pinot Noir. The Champenois, never a breed to miss a trick or two, also recognised the potential for fabulous fizz from New Zealand. Which is why Champagne Deutz joined up with Marlborough-based Montana (who independently make consistently good-quality, distinguished fizzes), invested a heap of money, and promptly produced the stunning Marlborough Deutz sparklers.

south africa

While quite a lot of South Africa's sparkling wine is made using the *cuve close* method (see page 19), which luckily for us is generally consumed within South Aftrica, a number of startlingly good bottle-fermented fizzes have begun to emerge. The South Africans have introduced their own sparkling wine term, Méthode Cap Classique, for these fizzes. The future looks temptingly promising, with some delicate, well-structured wines making their presence felt beyond the borders of the Cape. And what better indicator of this promise than the fact that the Champagne house of Mumm has already teamed up with one of the finest stars in this still tiny industry to produce Cuvée Cap by Mumm?

how to choose fizz

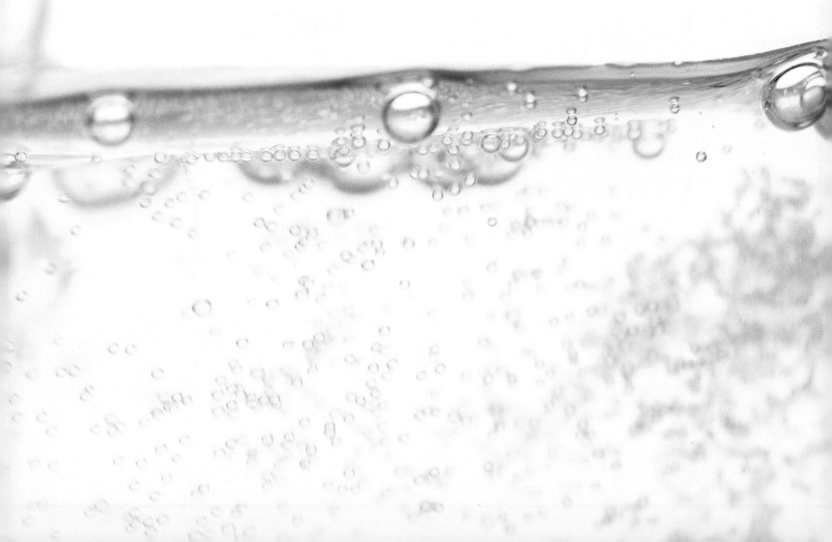

anytime, anywhere fizz

Medium-bodied, approachable and easy-drinking fizzes, with lots of upfront fruit, some richness, well-balanced and full of flavour. Great food fizzes.

the great thing about the fizzes I've selected for this section is that they are extremely versatile. Unlike the richer, heavier styles of fizz where a glass or two can be enough, these wines will see you through wherever you are and however long it lasts. Whether it's partying or lunching with friends, these fizzes will add just that touch of sparkle to all kinds of occasions. The growing trend for wine by the glass in bars and clubs means that it is easier to indulge in a glass of fizz without splashing out on a whole bottle. It's also a great way to discover some new fizzes... Should you know someone who's not keen on fizz, you can guarantee to convert them in no time with one of these fun and fizzy 'anytime, anywhere' wines.

These sparkling wines are very easy to drink, they just slip down beautifully. The added advantage is that they tend to be more widely available and offer great value for money too. What's more, they are great with food, having enough 'weight', body and depth of flavour to cope. Champagne Billecart-Salmon Brut Reserve NV with sea bass in a light cream and vanilla sauce is heavenly. And if you're munching on home-made hamburgers with a pile of hot chips, what other than an American bestseller – Korbel Brut NV?

breakfast and brunch

There's something wonderfully decadent about sipping bubbly at breakfast time. Imagine the smell of freshly brewed coffee and the sight of toasted muffins and scrambled eggs with smoked salmon. Why not spoil yourself and crack open a bottle of fizz? Even if you don't have friends round, do you really need an excuse to indulge on a late Sunday morning? I'm all for it! The clean, refreshing flavours of these medium-bodied fizzes, with their crisp acidity, are ideal to cut through the morning fuzz – and the creamy eggs. If you

prefer something refreshing and revitalizing, add fizz to a glass of orange juice to make Buck's Fizz (see page 109). For the best flavour, it is important to use freshly squeezed orange juice. It makes all the difference. For a special breakfast or brunch fizz, you can do no better than Champagne Perrier-Jouët NV. It has attractive balance, and lots of tangy fruit with a light vanilla finish. The lively S. Anderson Napa Valley Brut NV, with its tinglingly refreshing lemon-citrussy character, is a great Californian brunch fizz.

For more breakfast fizz suggestions, see page 90

on the town

Meeting up with friends at the end of a hard week at work? Stopping off at your favourite bar for a quick drink and gossip? Start the evening in style with a glass or two of fizz. Go for wines with some body and weight, and fruit character, something you can really savour and enjoy. I've found Champagne Gosset Brut Excellence NV, with its toasted aroma and tangy fruit, works wonders at getting everyone into the mood; and those bubbles are a wonderful reminder that the fun has started. The spicy apricot and sherbet overtones of the Californian Korbel Brut NV make it a winner every time. Why not try the house fizz if you know the place and enjoy the wines? And if you decide to order some food, hang on to that glass of fizz.

For more 'on the town' fizz suggestions, see page 56

STOP!
READ WARNING
BELOW

staying in

Curled up on the sofa with a good movie and a take-away – do you really need more of an excuse to share a bottle of fizz? After all, these are drink-me anytime anywhere fizzes, and sparkling wine is surprisingly good with Chinese noodles and spicy foods, not to mention fish and chips! Two great-value fizzes to pick up on the way home are the easy-drinking Angus Brut Pinot Noir Chardonnay NV from Australia and the Spanish Castell 1909 Cava NV. This relatively full-bodied cava, with its hint of liquorice and tangy yet creamy flavour on the finish, tastes more-ishly good with lots of ethnic dishes.

Here's a fail-safe recipe for those moments when you need pampering or cheering up. Pour a glass of fabulous fizz such as the Champagne Billecart-Salmon Rosé NV, with its delicate vanilla aroma and delicious mouthful of strawberries and cream. Now put on some favourite music. One of my favourite pieces, which always makes me laugh out loud, is Strauss's *The Champagne Polka*, complete with authentic-sounding popping corks.

For more 'staying in' fizz suggestions, see page 56

lunch

A glass of fizz can turn a simple lunch into a sparkly affair. After a morning's hard shopping, treat yourself to some bubbles with that plate of smoked salmon or stir-fried noodles. Gloria Ferrer Blanc de Noirs NV is a sensational fizz from California. Pale pink in colour, with red-fruit flavours, this is a great way to start a leisurely girls' lunch. The elegant Mumm de Cramant Grand Cru NV, with its toasty, buttery flavour, will slip down beautifully with salmon served in a variety of guises. The non-vintage Lindauer Special Reserve from New Zealand, with its unusual and attractive yeasty, slightly biscuity edge, makes a refreshing, gently uplifting lunchtime sparkler, while you can't go wrong with Angus Brut Rosé NV, a great everyday pink fizz from Australia.

For more lunchtime fizz suggestions, see pages 61 and 75

seduction

Domaine Carneros NV is a top-quality Californian sparkling wine that needs to be tasted to be believed. Made in conjunction with the Champagne house Taittinger, this is a really delicious fizz with

One of my favourite Australian fizzes at the moment is the raspberry and vanilla-tasting Yalumba Cuvée One Pinot Noir Chardonnay NV.

a creamy aroma and lots of red-fruit flavour. As my tasting notes on this fizz read, 'it has an extremely seductive after-taste'. This could well be one to pick if you have a hot new date! Billecart-Salmon Brut Réserve NV is an immensely classy Champagne, with a subtle and complex, creamy vanilla aroma. The combination of a chilled glass of this elegant fizz served with oysters in a shallot and vinegar dressing is exquisite, and, yes, I most certainly believe that together they are one of the most powerful aphrodisiacs around!

One very persuasive fizz to come out of South Africa is Cabriere Estate's Pierre Jourdan Cuvée Belle Rose NV. Made from 100% Pinot Noir it has just the faintest hint of pink, luscious soft fruit and a crisp finish. Lindauer Special Reserve NV is a great wine to serve at an intimate gathering, when there's just the two of you – or anytime when you want a relatively special sparkler to linger over without breaking the bank. This is one of New Zealand's most consistently good fizzes.

For more seductive fizz suggestions, see pages 58 and 84

For two intimates, lovers or comrades, to spend a quiet evening with a magnum, drinking no aperitif before, nothing but a glass of cognac after – that is the ideal.

... The worst time is that dictated by convention, in a crowd, in the early afternoon, at a wedding reception. Evelyn Waugh, *New York Vogue*, 1937

parties

All the best parties I have ever been to revolved around fizz. You don't, of course, have to have such a grand setting as Versailles (see page 10) for a fabulous party. But something about that pop of the cork really does conjure up an immediate party atmosphere, however informal or smart the setting. There is simply nothing like getting high on sparkling wine and what you'll notice at fizz-only parties is that the bubble doesn't seem to burst. I'm also convinced that if you stick to drinking only good fizz, you won't get a hangover.

There are lots of cool new happening drinks around, but if you are throwing a big birthday party, serving fizz and only fizz throughout has to be the coolest choice of all. A medium-bodied, fruity sparkling wine with a gentle acidity will be a very popular choice. Seaview Brut NV from Australia, with its slightly smoky aroma and gentle fruit, is a great inexpensive choice, particularly for big parties, while

the easy-drinking, crisply acid Korbel Brut NV is a good all-rounder. If your budget is more generous, the delicious ice-cream-soda-flavoured Champagne Mumm Cordon Rouge NV makes the perfect party fizz.

For parties where the emphasis is on food, especially if it includes seafood such as prawns or the more glamorous oysters, you cannot beat a decent bottle of medium-bodied Champagne. Veuve Clicquot Yellow Label NV, with its stylish yeasty aroma and creamy fruit, is a great foil for oysters. They were made for each other. If you like the thought of Champagne with a slightly toasted aroma, then serve Gosset Grande Réserve NV. It has lots of apricots and peachy flavours and a lovely tang of tropical fruit on the finish. As with many good non-vintage Champagnes, stash a few bottles away (if you can resist drinking it) and it will become

richer still over the next few years. My next suggestion is not Champagne, but it will look good, impress your guests, and flatter the food. It's another of my favourite Australian fizzes, the raspberry and vanilla-tasting Yalumba Cuvée One Pinot Noir Chardonnay NV. I always think its packaging looks a bit like the Champagne Bollinger RD Label; the fizz is almost as complex and classy too. **For more party fizz suggestions, see pages 61, 71 and 85**

outside/bbqs

If you have friends coming round for a barbecue, keep them entertained while the charcoal heats up by serving good, easy-drinking bubbly. The Aussies are, of course, masters of the barbecue, so it makes sense to me to serve some Australian fizz. One of my favourites is Green Point, a wine made in conjunction

The Nineties, the 'Gay Nineties', were the peak period of the popularity of Champagne in England. There was peace and plenty, profits and prospects for all and sundry as never before or since... What other wine than Champagne could be ordered on festive occasions, the gay foil of the bottle, the merry popping of the cork, the dancing bubbles in the glass helped all alike, making guests happy and articulate, hence the party a success.

André Simon, *Vintagewise*

with the Champagne house Moët & Chandon. While Green Point is a vintage wine – at the time of writing, the vintage is 1995 – (see also vintage fizzes, pages 80–95), it is consistently good, with a lovely intense, slightly toasted aroma, and excellent balanced fruit. It's an extremely more-ish fizz with all that delicious fruit flavour, which makes it just perfect to keep everyone from starving as they wait for the food!

Another good bet from Australia is the value-for-money Angus Brut Pinot Noir Chardonnay NV, which has lots of violet-like floral fruit. This tastes very good with marinated or herby meat, or with fish. If you fancy some pink fizz how about trying Lindauer Brut Rosé NV, tangy with lots of black cherry flavours? Latecomers don't have to miss out on a glass either, as this New Zealand fizz is good with barbecued fish such as salmon, as well as with vegetable kebabs or tangy marinated chicken.

Certain cavas seem to have the right amount of almost smoky fruit themselves to complement barbecued food, and are particularly delicious with garlicky foods. I can highly recommend the Castell 1909 Cava NV with barbecued chicken and trout, or with anything served in a sweet and sour barbecue sauce.

For more barbecue fizz suggestions, see pages 8 and 61

picnics

Whether you are planning a lazy late picnic lunch or are off with a crowd on one of those pick-and-mix affairs where everyone brings what they want, a medium-bodied fizz is the perfect choice to keep everyone buzzing. One of my favourite Champagnes

The California
fizz, Domaine
Carneros NV, offers
a wonderful
summertime glass
of red-fruit
creamy fizz.

for taking to picnics is the Jacquart Brut Mosaïque NV, which has lots of elegant raspberry and violet-like fruit flavours on the palate. It always evokes for me the taste of fresh summer berries and summer pudding and therefore seems a good suggestion for picnics or indeed any outdoor entertaining. A grape variety that always makes me think of summer is Chenin Blanc, used to make Vouvray in the Loire Valley. It has a slightly honeyed aroma and is highly perfumed. One of my favourite Vouvrays is the Marc Brédif Brut Vouvray, which I would thoroughly recommend. The Californian fizz, Domaine Carneros NV, offers a wonderful summer-time glass of red-fruit creamy fizz.

In England, open-air concerts ending with fireworks have become increasingly popular. At one wonderful concert I went to with friends at Highclere Castle in Berkshire, we enjoyed an amazing picnic supper of salmon, quails' eggs and lobster, washed down with magnums of chilled Champagne Heidsieck Monopole NV (see also aperitif-style fizzes, pages 54–67). Even the light shower of rain didn't spoil the dry tangy fruit and the subtle, quite rich lemon-meringue flavours on the finish of this fabulous fizz. To give your picnic a touch of style, pack some bottles of Champagne Mumm de Cramant Grand Cru NV. Made from 100% Chardonnay grapes, this has a lovely toasted aroma and hints of buttery, slightly smoky fruit. Try it and discover how well it partners everything from prawns to spicy sausages.

But, more often than not, you're there for the fun, the music and the party atmosphere – the fizz is the added bonus.

Dare to be different and pour pink fizz, such as the Californian Korbel Brut Rosé NV, with its delicious raspberry-like aroma and flavour.

The easy-drinking, good-value Seaview Brut NV is another winner for a picnic, while for a really refreshing pink fizz, I'd serve Lindauer Brut Rosé NV. It's a great bargain, with a tangy black-cherry flavour. You can happily drink it with anything. Whatever you choose, make sure your fizz is well chilled before you set out. It might not look very elegant, but wrapping the cold bottles in newspaper will keep the fizz perfectly cool. You can of course use one of the more glamorous Champagne cooler-sleeves, which fit snugly around the bottle – practical for taking on picnics.

For more picnic fizzes, see page 65

supper parties

For those occasions when you are having a relaxed supper, a medium-bodied bubbly is often the best choice. No-one's in a hurry; there's plenty of time before sitting down to eat to savour a glass or two of fruity, easy-drinking fizz such as the S. Anderson Napa Valley Brut NV. Dare to be different and pour pink fizz, such as the Korbel Brut Rosé NV, with its delicious raspberry-like aroma and flavour. If you fancy continuing with the fizz throughout the meal, a rosé can be a good bet, especially if you are eating lamb, pork, chicken or fish. Champagne Louis

Roederer Brut Rosé NV is very pale pink, with a light, elegant, tangy fruit flavour and an aftertaste to die for – raspberries and cream. I've enjoyed both rosés with new-season English lamb and redcurrant jelly. The red-fruit flavours in the fizzes seem to accentuate the sweetness of the jelly.

Even the simplest suppers suddenly become more exciting with an accompanying glass of fizz. Korbel Brut NV, for example, goes surprisingly well with hamburgers – its crisp acidity neatly cutting through the richness of the dish. A plate of cold salmon with hollandaise is magically transformed by the relatively rich Champagne Billecart-Salmon Rosé NV. Its sister white fizz, Billecart-Salmon Brut Réserve NV, makes a regular appearance in my house. It's the wonderful balance of lightly toasted fruit and elegance that makes this fizz so sexy. Try it with fish and cream sauces; it's sensational. Joseph Perrier Cuvée Royale NV is another favourite Champagne of mine. It's a sort of gentle apple-pie-like fizz which is elegant yet flavoursome enough to complement a whole range of starters, from artichokes and asparagus (both supposedly difficult to match with wine) to pan-fried scallops.

For more supper-party fizz suggestions, see pages 61 and 76

All the best parties I have ever been to revolved around fizz.
There is simply nothing like getting high on Champagne and

what you'll notice at fizz-only parties is that the bubble doesn't seem to burst – everyone remains on a high all evening.

weddings

Fabulous fizz is an absolute must, whether for a small family affair or a grand, formal reception. Guests will be more than delighted with a fruity, easy-drinking yet stylish fizz. There are lots of favourite Champagnes that I can recommend. Moët & Chandon NV always shows well, with its creamy nose and almost sweet apple-like flavour. Billecart-Salmon Brut Réserve NV has always been one of my favourite wedding Champagnes. Another good fizz to drink throughout a wedding reception is the toasty Gosset Brut Excellence NV. Its very tangy fruit flavour always makes it a most welcome and lively choice.

Wedding fizz does not have to be expensive. On a warm summer's day, why not try the gently honeyed, perfumed Brut Vouvray from Marc Brédif? Yalumba Cuvée One Pinot Noir Chardonnay NV is a deliciously stylish fizz from Australia, with tempting raspberry and vanilla flavours. Should you wish to add a splash of colour to the event and offer Kir Royale too (see page 109), those soft summer fruit flavours are a perfect foil for the cassis. Just as impressive is the Californian Domaine Carneros NV; its creamy texture is a real treat. I often think a sparkling rosé makes a fabulous wedding fizz, especially one as stylish as the strawberry-flavoured Etoile Rosé NV, from California's Domaine Chandon. When it comes to a toast for the newly-weds, the question of what to offer is easily solved – bring out a vintage fizz and keep the bubbles rising... (see pages 80–95).

For more wedding fizz suggestions, see pages 10, 65, 72 and 86

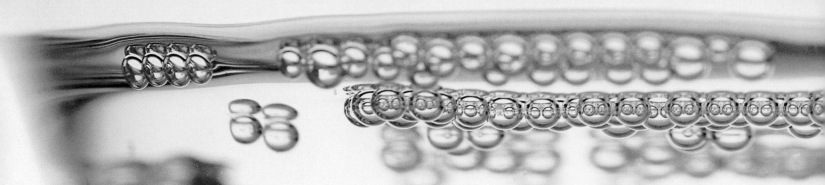

taste notes

A quick reference guide to the best medium-bodied fizzes

France – Champagne

Billecart-Salmon Brut Réserve NV *'Subtle, complex, with creamy vanilla flavours'*

Georges Gardet Cuvée Flavy NV *'Yeasty, with lots of tangy fruit'*

Gosset Brut Excellence NV *'Toasted aroma and tangy fruit'*

Gosset Grande Réserve NV *'Apricots and peaches with a tropical-fruit finish'*

Jacquart Brut Mosaïque NV *'Elegant, with raspberry and violet fruit'*

Joseph Perrier Cuvée Royale NV *'Elegant, apple-pie-like Champagne'*

Moët & Chandon NV *'Creamy, with a hint of sweet apples'*

Mumm Cordon Rouge NV *'Ice-cream-soda Champagne'*

Mumm de Cramant Grand Cru NV *'Elegant, with a toasty, buttery flavour'*

Perrier-Jouët NV *'Tangy fizz with light vanilla on the finish'*

Piper Heidsieck NV *'Honeyed, with creamy caramel-like fruit'*

Veuve Clicquot Yellow Label NV *'Stylish, creamy fizz'*

France – Rosé Champagne

Billecart-Salmon Rosé NV *'Delicate, with strawberries-and-cream flavours'*

Louis Roederer Brut Rosé NV *'Light, elegant raspberries-and-cream rosé'*

France – Loire

Marc Brédif Brut Vouvray *'Subtly perfumed with honeyed flavours'*

California

Domaine Carneros NV *'Delicious red fruit creamy fizz'*

Korbel Brut NV *'Easy-drinking fizz with spicy apricot and sherbet overtones'*

S. Anderson Napa Valley Brut NV *'Lemon-sherbet-like, with hints of pear'*

California – Rosé

Gloria Ferrer Blanc de Noirs NV *'Very pale pink with red-fruit flavours'*

Domaine Carneros Rosé NV *'Delicious raspberry-ripple-flavoured fizz'*

Domaine Chandon Etoile Rosé NV *'Stylish strawberry-like fizz'*

Korbel Brut Rosé NV *'Elegant fizz with masses of mouthwatering raspberry fruit'*

Australia

Angus Brut Pinot Noir Chardonnay NV *'Floral, with violet-like fruit'*

Seaview Brut NV *'Smoky aroma, creamy palate, good value'*

Yaldara Reserve Brut NV *'Light, appley, elderflower party fizz'*

Yalumba Cuvée One Pinot Noir Chardonnay NV *'Complex, with raspberry and vanilla flavours'*

Australia – Rosé

Angus Brut Rosé NV *'Great everyday easy-drinking pink fizz'*

New Zealand

Lindauer Special Reserve NV *'Unusual, yeasty, biscuity, creamy fizz'*

New Zealand – Rosé

Lindauer Brut Rosé NV *'Black-cherry-like tangy fruit'*

Spain

Castell 1909 Cava NV *'White chocolate aroma with tangy liquorice and cream on the finish'*

South Africa

Cabriere Estate Pierre Jourdan Cuvée Belle Rose NV *'Softly fruity, with good balancing acidity'*

the ultimate aperitif

Light-bodied and elegant, crisp and appley, subtle in flavour, ideal for drinking on their own or as an aperitif with food.

fizz is an exhilarating drink; being greeted with a welcome glass of sparkling wine can magically transform the mood into one of celebration. To achieve this sparkling sensation calls for what I describe as the 'aperitif-style' fizz. If you like your fizz subtle, this style is for you. Light and elegant, these bubblies taste sensational on their own, work wonders at breaking the ice and making introductions at parties, and will get everyone fizzing.

The great thing about serving a fizz as an aperitif is that you don't have to mess about with spirits, mixers, ice or lemon. All you need are some decent glasses (see pages 134–137) and to ensure that the wine is well chilled. I find that fizz poured from magnums always makes an impressive aperitif.

There's a whole host of fizzes in this section to suit all pockets and preferences – I guarantee you'll discover some wonderful wines to share with your friends (or keep for yourself...). While many of these aperitif-style fizzes are wonderful on their own, they often have enough 'weight' of fruit to be equally fabulous with lighter foods. I've suggested occasions where you might enjoy a glass of sparkling wine in isolated splendour – perhaps at the bar while waiting for your friends to arrive – and times when you can happily drink these subtle fizzes with all kinds of delicious food.

bars and restaurants

Waiting for the rest of the crowd to gather, or enjoying a quiet drink before moving on to a restaurant for supper? In anticipation of a good evening, I'd go for a glass of refreshing fizz every time. One of the great things about the bar and restaurant scene now is the increasingly wide range of fizzes you can choose by the glass. Look out for Lindauer Brut NV; this is consistently good and, with its unusual hint of melons and its dry, crisply fruity character, is bound to revive your tastebuds! Cuvée Napa by Mumm Brut NV, with its apple-sherbet aroma and flavour, makes a great alternative. But if you fancy the real thing – and why not? – then Champagne Heidsieck Monopole NV is the one. Light, elegant and appley, this gentle fizz always goes down extremely well.

For more bar and restaurant fizz suggestions, see page 34

taking a bottle

A good bottle of fizz is the ideal choice to take round to friends. Whether it's for a dinner party or just popping round for a drink, you can guarantee everyone will appreciate a fizzing aperitif. The light, sherbet-like Champagne Lanson Black Label Brut NV is a foolproof choice; and it slips down well with crunchy crudités and dips. An affordable yet tasty, light aperitif suitable for all palates is the Australian fizz, Yaldara Reserve Brut Rosé NV.

just because...

For those moments when you quite simply fancy some fabulous fizz. The ultimate luxury has to be a deep steaming-hot bath and a glass of foaming fizz. My favourite for sipping in the bath is Pol Roger White Foil NV, one of the finest light Champagnes around at

the moment. There's something quite decadent about rosé fizz, too. California's Codorníu Napa Rosé NV, with its delicate aroma and flavour of strawberries and raspberries, always seems to hit the spot.

The choices here are endless and really depend on your mood. For exceptional value for money, I find top cavas from Spain are a good bet and much more pleasant to drink than a nondescript (probably acidic) Champagne at the same price. Two mouth-wateringly good examples are Codorníu Cuvée Raventós NV and Freixenet Cordón Negro NV (both come in distinctive bottles too). The easy-drinking Raventós is light, yet complex, with a

creamy nose and floral, soft fruit, while the black-bottled Cordón Negro has an enticing aroma, apple-sherbet-like fruit, and a hint of apricot and melon on the finish.

Sometimes in the late afternoon, when I'm not sure if I'm in 'savoury' or 'sweet' mode, a chilled glass of an Italian fizz such as the exquisitely fragrant Moscato d'Asti from Marco Negri (see page 103 for more producers) is a wonderful solution. With its hint of sweetness on the finish, this style of fizz makes a delicious thirst-quencher.

For more recommended fizzes for those particular moments, see page 35

the two of you

Any romantic liaison, or indeed one you hope might develop into an affair to remember, has to involve some fabulous fizz. It is, after all, *the* romantic drink and nothing can beat an elegant flute of bubbly as the aperitif to a special evening. Champagne Pol Roger White Foil NV has to be my first choice. It has a lovely elegant aroma with hints of ginger and cream, a perfect balance with good acidity, and a delicious finish. My tasting notes for this favourite fizz simply read 'liquid sex in a bottle'. Enough said!

THE SOUND OF THY
EXPLOSIVE CORK,
CHAMPAGNE, HAS, BY SOME
STRANGE WITCHERY, OF A
SUDDEN TAUGHT MEN THE
SWEET MUSIC OF SPEECH.
A MURMUR AS OF A RISING
STORM RUNS ROUND THE
TABLE: BADINAGE COMMENCES,
FLIRTATIONS FLOURISH…
WE MIGHT TELL OF
BREAKFASTS, AND OF
SUPPERS, SUDDENLY
CONVERTED FROM SAHARAS
OF INTOLERABLE DULLNESS
INTO OASES OF SMILES AND
LAUGHTER BY THE
APPEARANCE OF CHAMPAGNE.

Charles Tovey, *Wit, Wisdom and Morals, Distilled from Bacchus*

But don't worry, not every date has to be expensive. Good-value pink bubbly can make quite an impression too. One of my favourite Californian sparkling wines is the delicious Cuvée Napa by Mumm Rosé NV. A wonderful pale pink, crisp and floral with lots of easy-drinking fruit, this is a consistently good fizz.

For more romantic fizz suggestions, see pages 35 and 84

lazy lunches

If you've got friends coming for lunch – particularly for a barbecue or the kind of help-yourself-affair that lingers on through the afternoon – get things off to a gentle start by serving a good aperitif-style fizz. The southern French fizz Blanquette de Limoux, Plan Pujade, with its attractively aromatic flavours, or a lemony, lightly honeyed fizz from the Loire Valley's Saumur region would both be a good bet. Try the gently frothing Bouvet Saumur Brut, which has lots of soft, floral fruit and thirst-quenching crispness.

Gloria Ferrer Sonoma Brut NV, with its attractive hints of apples and herbs, is a fabulous lunchtime aperitif fizz. Lighter-style Californian fizzes like this one have just the right amount of upfront fruit to cope with food as well as offering a delicious mouthful on their own.

Cava is an ideal choice to get everyone in the mood. A classic aperitif-style fizz that is delicious on its own, it has the distinctive flavours to taste good even with spicy eats like garlic-laced olives. Try Sandora Blanc de Blancs Cava Brut NV, with its elegant, earthy fruit and hint of butter on the finish.

For more lazy lunchtime fizz suggestions, see page 35

all-day parties

Fizz always goes down well at parties, particularly early in the day when you need a lift, yet fancy something gentle. The light, refreshing aperitif-style fizzes are ideal, and the good news is that lots of the less expensive fizzes come into their own here, particularly for making Buck's Fizz. A very good party option is Asti Spumante. Light in style (and lower in alcohol), with soft acidity and that hint of sweetness on the finish, it's ideal for sipping on its own. Next time you throw a small party, treat everyone to an Asti Spumante such as Bruno Giacosa Spumante Classico Extra Brut (see page 103 for more producers).

If you enjoy light, soft fizzes, why not try a Loire Valley sparkling wine made from the Chenin Blanc grape, such as Langlois Crémant de Loire? This soft, honeyed, floral French fizz, with its elderflower-like finish, is the ideal, gentle aperitif, especially when too much acidity would be a shock to the palate (and stomach). Chenin Blanc is a good complement to all sorts of tasty aperitif foods and tastes especially good with smoked trout pâté on melba toasts, crudités and mushroom or tomato tartlets.

An aperitif-style cava can be a good bet. One of my favourites is the Rondel Premier Cuvée Brut NV, which is light, tangy and floral, and easy to drink. For those of you who can't leave the peanuts and pretzels alone, it's worth remembering that these crisp, refreshingly acid fizzes are a good foil for salty nibbles. For a touch of style, the refreshing Champagne Lanson Black Label Brut NV will set the tone for the rest of the party. Or serve a glass of the easy-drinking party Champagne, Mercier NV. Another great party fizz is the Australian

Yaldara Reserve Brut NV. If you fancy something pink that isn't as expensive as Champagne, you can't go wrong with Australian fizz such as the Seppelt Great Western Brut Rosé NV. This tastes particularly good with tasty little fish nibbles such as prawns, oysters, little fish tarts or miniature smoked salmon quiches.

For more party fizz suggestions, see pages 40 and 71

sunday lunches

Sunday lunch with the family in my house is legendary. It's not really surprising when you consider I have eight brothers and sisters, not to mention a similar number of hangers-on (our irreverent term for the in-laws). With so many fizz fans in the family, we invariably start with a glass of bubbly. Champagne Heidsieck Monopole NV is light, elegant and appley and always goes down well. For such big gatherings, how about trying one of my favourite Californian fizzes, Cuvée Napa by Mumm Rosé NV, crisp and floral with red fruit overtones? This has the added advantage of being around half the price of its Champagne counterpart. These fizzes taste good with smoked salmon on brown bread or crostini, garlic croûtons with pesto, and cherry tomatoes with goats' cheese and basil.

supper

For simple relaxed suppers with friends, you can't go wrong with a glass of pick-me-up fizz to begin the evening. The light, easy-drinking Gloria Ferrer Sonoma Brut NV from California is a good bet, as is an Australian fizz such as the appley Yaldara Reserve Brut NV. Another Aussie favourite is Cockatoo Ridge Brut NV, which

has an attractive sherbet-like flavour and good acidity. Either serve these Aussie fizzes on their own or simply add a drop of crème de cassis to make a Kir Royale, an attractively coloured tasty blackcurrant-flavoured fizzy aperitif (see page 109). A dramatic choice of aperitif and so easy to make, but at least it will look as though you made an effort!

For more relaxed supper fizz suggestions, see page 47

celebratory dinner

A celebration is a reason to treat yourself. Nothing beats a glass of fabulous fizz for making you feel special. If you want some seriously good rosé Champagne and can persuade some generous-hearted relative or friend to give you a bottle, nothing is finer than Krug Rosé NV. It is simply exquisite, a deliciously light aperitif-style Champagne. Extremely pale in colour, it has a wonderful delicate balance of red-fruit flavours. Alternatively, serve flutes of the delicious Pol Roger White Foil NV or the strawberry-fruited R. de Ruinart Brut NV – both elegant, refined and stylish Champagnes.

There are plenty of class acts to choose from outside Champagne too. Lindauer is astounding value for money. Several times over the years I have blind-tasted this alongside many non-vintage Champagnes that cost three times the price and this New Zealand beauty has triumphed. With an unusual aroma of melons and a crisp tangy, refreshing apple-like flavour, this fizz always proves to be a talking point. It's a superb aperitif and will ensure any dinner gets off to a bubbly start. South Africa is beginning to yield some really exciting sparkling wines in the classic 'Champagne' style. Krone Borealis Brut NV, Cape Classique is a fabulous combination of gentle fruit and good acidity, making it an ideal – and unexpected – choice to serve at a special dinner.

I'm only a beer teetotaller, not a champagne teetotaller.

George Bernard Shaw, *Candida*

Delicately pale Champagne Piper Heidsieck Rosé NV –
perfect with prawns, smoked salmon or red onion tartlets.

al fresco

All the best outdoor meals – whatever time of day or evening they begin – start off with a glass of fizz. Even if the sun isn't shining, fizz can lighten up the atmosphere. I have wonderful memories of a wet summer's day, thanks to the light, vanilla-sherbet Champagne Canard-Duchêne NV we were drinking! For a change, why not try a Crémant from Alsace, with its floral, almost spicy character and gentle fizz? Dopff 'au Moulin' Cuvée Julien NV, Crémant d'Alsace, has lots of perfumed fruit – just right for sipping in the garden, in the company of friends, on a hot summer's day.

While vines have been planted in England since Roman times, we haven't in the past had a reputation for producing any serious bubblies. That, however, has now changed with the arrival of Nyetimber Blanc de Blancs 1995 and Chapel Down Epoch Brut NV. The latter is rather distinctive, with an unusual ginger and elderflower-like aroma and flavour. You'll either love it or hate it. Just one whiff of this fizz reminds me of the smell of summer flowers and freshly cut grass.

For more al fresco fizz suggestions, see pages 42 and 75

weddings

You simply can't have a decent wedding without some really good fizz to greet the thirsty guests. Good Champagne is, of course, delicious. Laurent-Perrier is one of my favourite wedding fizzes, dry with a steely, 'green apple' aroma. It is a very elegant, stylish fizz, and you will find guests will have no problem at all drinking it as they mingle. Rosé makes an interesting choice of aperitif. The delicately pale Champagne Piper Heidsieck Rosé NV, with its unusual violet-like aroma, would be ideal. It tastes good on its own but also goes well with all kinds of light foods, such as Champagne Prawns (see page 116), smoked salmon, mini kebabs and little red onion tarts.

Offering fizz to welcome the guests doesn't have to mean saving up for months. There are lots of good, light-style, affordable bubblies around. Look no further than the Gloria Ferrer Sonoma Brut NV, or pour a cava such as Codorníu Cuvée Raventós NV. With its distinctive floral flavours, cava is a real crowd-pleasing aperitif-style fizz and ideal to serve with canapés, too.

For more wedding fizz suggestions, see pages 10, 51, 72 and 86

taste notes

A quick reference guide to the best aperitif-style fizzes

France – Champagne

R. de Ruinart Brut NV *'Light, elegant strawberry fruit'*

Canard-Duchêne NV *'Subtle, with vanilla and sherbet'*

Heidsieck Monopole NV *'Light, elegant, apple sherbet'*

Mercier NV *'Easy-drinking party fizz'*

Pol Roger White Foil NV *'Elegant, perfectly balanced with hints of ginger and cream'*

Lanson Black Label Brut NV *'Light and sherbet-like'*

Laurent-Perrier NV *'Stylish, crisp, apple-citrus flavours'*

France – Rosé Champagne

Piper Heidsieck Rosé NV *'Unusual, violet-like aroma and flavour'*

Krug Rosé NV *'Very pale colour, exquisite red-fruit flavour'*

Rest of France

Langlois Crémant de Loire *'Soft, gentle, floral elderflower-like fizz'*

Dopff 'au Moulin' Cuvée Julien, Crémant d'Alsace *'Light, tangy-perfumed fruit'*

Blanquette de Limoux, Plan Pujade *'Aromatic, with a hint of cream'*

Bouvet Saumur Brut *'Soft, honeyed-floral fruit'*

California

Cuvée Napa by Mumm Brut NV *'Apple-sherbet aroma and flavour'*

Gloria Ferrer Sonoma Brut NV *'Light, easy-drinking, with overtones of apples and herbs'*

California – Rosé

Cuvée Napa by Mumm Rosé NV *'Crisp and floral with red-fruit overtones'*

Codorníu Napa Rosé NV *'Delicate, with hints of strawberries and raspberries'*

Australia

Yaldara Reserve Brut NV *'Party wine, with appley, elderflower flavour'*

Cockatoo Ridge Brut NV *'Dry, tangy-sherbet-like fizz'*

Australia – Rosé

Yaldara Reserve Brut Rosé NV *'Dry, tangy aperitif'*

Seaview Brut Rosé NV *'Dry and tangy, with lots of red-fruit flavours'*

Seppelt Great Western Brut Rosé NV *'Violet-like nose with mouth-watering, more-ish fruit'*

New Zealand

Lindauer Brut NV *'Unusual hint of melons with a dry, crisp-apple flavour'*

Spain

Codorníu Cuvée Raventós NV *'Complex creamy nose with a floral perfumed aftertaste'*

Freixenet Cordón Negro NV *'Apple sherbet-like fruit, with a hint of apricot and melon'*

Rondel Premier Cuvée Cava Brut NV *'Tangy fruit flavour and slight caramel on the finish'*

Sandora Blanc de Blancs Cava Brut NV *'Elegant, earthy fruit, with a hint of butter on the finish'*

England

Chapel Down Epoch Brut NV *'Unusual ginger and elderflower-like aroma and flavour'*

South Africa

Krone Borealis Brut NV, Cap Classique *'Elegant, fresh and softly fruity'*

the ultimate party

For a party that draws attention, make sure you serve a fizz that demands attention. For the truly extravagant among you, Krug Grand Cuvée NV served in magnums is the ultimate party Champagne. I doubt you'll find your friends will turn down the offer of a chilled glass of Champagne Bollinger Special Cuvée NV either. 'Bolly' has gained glamorous infamy as the fizz without which Patsy (played by the actress Joanna Lumley) could not function in the UK television sitcom *Absolutely Fabulous*. This is a big wine, with complex strawberry-like aromas and a long apples, pears and caramel aftertaste. A glass of this on its own is very very good. For a stylish Champagne that is brilliant value for money (and thus perfect for big parties), offer Champagne Georges Gardet Brut Spécial NV. It's rich, with quite creamy fruit and lots of red-berry flavours; and it always receives rave reviews.

Of course it doesn't have to be Champagne to be a fabulous party fizz. There are plenty of affordable sparkling wines with the richness, class and style for any fashion-conscious party. Deutz Marlborough Cuvée NV from New Zealand is great value. Zippy and invigorating, with an unusual honeycomb aroma and lots of creamy fruit, this makes a sensational party fizz. Or how about trying the Spanish Raimat Grand Brut NV, which is a stunning food fizz? This cava has tiny bubbles with an attractive, rich, almost sweet aroma and rich, creamy fruit on the palate. It's a

I suppose the obvious celebration at which to bring out richer fizzes is the wedding meal – be it brunch, lunch or dinner. I'm all in favour of drinking fizz right through the reception, and simply moving on from the lighter, aperitif-style fizz to these bigger, richer wines during the meal. Domaine Chandon's Cuvée 2000 NV, from the California arm of champagne house Moët & Chandon, is a perfect choice. It's rich, creamy and elegant, and a perfect partner to dishes such as turbot with a vanilla cream sauce. Should you prefer a red meat dish, then Korbel Blanc de Noirs NV may be the answer – certainly an unusual combination but a memorable one, which is what it's all about.

For more celebratory fizz suggestions, see pages 10, 51, 65 and 84

a very special evening

For these occasions, fizz is the magical answer. Whether in the garden for a late supper, dining on the terrace at your favourite restaurant and watching the sun go down, or picnicking at a grand open-air concert, why not make an occasion of it and enjoy some fabulous fizz? This is where the richer styles of fizz really comes into their own, as they have the weight and fruit to shine through all kinds of foods – spicy or creamy, meat or fish, savoury or sweet.

My first choice would be Champagne Charles Heidsieck Brut Reserve NV. It's a very good food wine, with its rich honeycomb aroma and almost sweet brioche flavour. If you look carefully at the neck label you'll see the words *'Mis en Cave 1993'* which means the bottle was laid down in the company's cellars in 1993. This new style of labelling tells you how much bottle age your non-vintage Champagne has had – generally the longer the bottle age, the richer the wine (see page 129 on how to lay down fizz). Another fizz with that wonderful honeycomb character is the stylish Korbel Chardonnay NV from California. Rich and buttery, this tastes great with spicy, creamy chicken dishes and will happily stay the pace of any outdoor event, grand or intimate.

For more special fizz suggestions, see pages 42 and 58

summer lunches

One of the many great things about fizz is that you can choose your glass to match the occasion and even the season. Think summer time. An ideal Californian fizz for glorious summer days is Mumm Napa Valley Blanc de Blancs NV. Made entirely from Chardonnay grapes, this wine at first appears light and elegant, but has weighty

Burgundy for kings,
Champagne for duchesses,
and claret for gentlemen.
French proverb

rich, buttery fruit on the palate and aftertaste. This is fabulous on its own, and with creamy chicken or pasta dishes, turbot, or char-grilled or roasted peppers. Another fizz I'd recommend is Spain's Raimat Grand Brut NV. Rich in flavour and texture, it retains the classic cava acidity and bite that make it simply perfect as a refreshing yet impressive lunchtime fizz.

Some types of smoked fish such as salmon, trout or even mackerel can obliterate the flavour of many lighter fizzes. But you'll find richer fizzes will be perfect. Champagne Joseph Perrier Blanc de Blancs Brut NV has an enticing buttery nose, with balanced rich, creamy flavours. This tastes excellent with smoked mackerel pâté served with horseradish sauce. If you are fond of pink fizz, why not try the rich Champagne Canard-Duchêne Rosé NV, which has lots of mouth-watering red-fruit flavours? As well as tasting

good with salmon, turbot and lamb, this fizz is delicious served with any red fruit or tangy summer fruit dessert.

For more summer fizz suggestions, see page 65

winter dining
Your first reaction might be to reach for a big, flavoursome red wine. But for a special dinner, think again. Have you ever tried fizz with coq au vin? Even though this dish is cooked using red wine, a rich, full-bodied fizz can still shine. Nautilus Marlborough Cuvée NV from New Zealand has just the right amount of toasted, rich and creamy fruit on the finish to complement this dish. Champagne Deutz Brut Classic NV has a wonderfully intense aroma with an almost meaty, yeasty flavour that makes the perfect partner for poultry; it tastes really good served with chicken,

poussin and guinea fowl. So, too, does the deliciously rich, biscuity Domaine Carneros Etoile NV from California.

Again, don't forget the pink fizz. Champagne Gosset Grand Rosé NV is a real showstopper, rich and concentrated, almost sweet on the nose, with ripe red-fruit flavours. Such is the staying power of this fizz, that you can successfully serve it with Thai spicy fish soup, Singapore noodles and many other oriental dishes that sometimes tax their wine partners. For a combination that will make the evening truly memorable, try this. Champagne Taittinger Prestige Rosé NV with juicy pink roast beef, lightly grilled calves liver or roast lamb with rosemary. This pink fizz is rich, full-bodied, with lots of upfront fruit flavour, and definitely powerful enough to serve in such company.

For more dinner-party fizz suggestions, see pages 47, 63 and 87

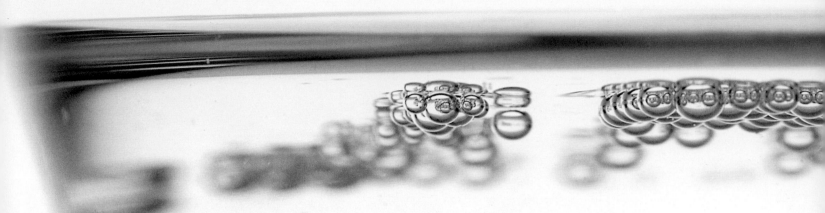

taste notes

A quick reference guide to the best full-bodied fizzes

France – Champagne

Bollinger Spécial Cuvée NV *'Rich, complex, with apple, caramel and cream flavours'*

Canard-Duchêne Prestige Cuvée Charles VII NV *'Apples and cream fizz'*

Charles Heidsieck Brut Resérve, Mis en Cave 1993 *'Honeycomb aroma and flavour, rich, with a hint of swee...*

Deutz Brut Classic NV *'Full-bodied, with intense yeasty fruit and flavour'*

Georges Gardet Brut Special NV *'Creamy with the flavour of red berries'*

Joseph Perrier Blanc de Blancs Brut NV *'Complex, with buttery, creamy nuances'*

Krug Grande Cuvée NV *'Complex, with creamy vanilla fruit and hints of apples and pears'*

Louis Roederer Brut Premier NV *'Smoky, rich, complex and restrained'*

France – Rosé Champagne

Canard-Duchêne Rosé NV *'Caramel aromas, with mouthwatering red-fruit flavours'*

Gosset Grand Rosé NV *'Rich and concentrated, with strawberry aromas and flavours'*

Taittinger Prestige Rosé NV *'Tangy and full-bodied, with redcurrant flavours'*

California

Codorníu Napa Brut NV *'Raspberry and vanilla-ice-cream flavours'*

Mumm Napa Valley Blanc de Blancs NV *'Complex, with rich buttery fruit'*

Domaine Carneros Etoile NV *'deliciously rich and biscuity'*

Domaine Chandon Cuvée 2000 NV, Late Disgorged *'Rich and creamy honeycomb-like fizz'*

Korbel Chardonnay NV *'Rich and buttery, with honeycomb aftertaste'*

California – Rosé

Korbel Blanc de Noirs NV *'Intense red-fruit flavours reminiscent of summer pudding'*

New Zealand

Deutz Marlborough Cuvée NV *'Honeycomb aroma and sherbet, creamy-like fruit'*

Nautilus Marlborough Cuvée NV *'Toasted, rich and creamy fruit'*

Spain

Raimat Grand Brut NV *'Fine mousse with rich, creamy fruit'*

just the two of you

What could be more romantic than sharing a bottle of Champagne, especially super-special vintage Champagne? Perrier-Jouët's Belle Epoque 1996 is seductive with its intense aroma and flavours of apricots and cream and whenever I have opened this wine, the stylish art nouveau bottle is lusted after almost as much as the contents! Joseph Perrier's stunning Cuvée Josephine 1995 is housed in an equally attractive colourful painted bottle. Despite its name, this is guaranteed not to induce the comment 'not tonight Josephine'! It's a rich, complex wine with an enticing pears and cream flavour – I defy anyone not to be seduced by it.

Duval-Leroy is making stunning Champagne and their vintage wines particularly impressed me. Try their Authentis, Trépail 1999 which is intensely rich with creamy nuances or the Authentis, Cumières 2000, a really unusual, lighter fizz with minty, floral characteristics and a touch of sweetness on the finish. A friend of mine recently proposed to his girlfriend over a bottle of Billecart-Salmon Rosé 1996. There was no way she could say no after just one sip of this classy fizz, which tastes like summer pudding in a glass. And the aftertaste goes on and on. Hope he's got lots of this in his cellar for the future... The Jacquart

Rosé 2000 is also a favourite of mine and will entrance anyone who loves full-bodied wines with its honeyed and caramel like flavour. It tastes absolutely delicious with dark chocolate.

For more romantic fizz suggestions, see pages 35 and 58

celebrations

Special 'milestones' in life demand a good vintage Champagne. I recently tasted Taittinger Comtes de Champagne, Blancs de Blancs 1996 at a christening and was really impressed with its elegant, perfumed aroma and mouth-watering red fruit flavour. I think this fabulous fizz received every bit as much attention as the baby! Another favourite for wetting the baby's head is the stunning Bruno Paillard 1996, a full-bodied wine with intense richness and a moreish aftertaste of raspberries. Laurent-Perrier 1996 is an equally full-bodied winner with stylish honeycomb-like flavours and a touch of dried apricots on the finish. Baby girls, of course, provide a really good excuse to open some top class vintage rosés. The Moët & Chandon Rosé 1999 is unusual with its hazelnuts and cream flavour and the Deutz Rosé 2000 is another good contender with equally unusual flavoursome overtones of rhubarb and sherbert on the finish. There is no more apt wine to serve at a

Golden Wedding anniversary celebration than the Heidsieck Gold Top 1997. This is a stunning wine with a rich golden colour and creamy pear-like character. And it is fantastic value too – you can buy at least three bottles of this to one bottle of other prestige cuvées. Pol Roger Cuvée Sir Winston Churchill 1995 is one of the most majestic Champagnes I've ever tasted and regal enough for even the grandest occasion. It is easy to understand why the great man himself was so partial to the wines from the Epernay-based house Pol Roger. Rich with luscious fruit, it has an enticing aroma and flavour of apricots with a hint of white chocolate and ginger. This is a complex wine that reveals new flavours with every sip.

If you want something more unusual for a fun birthday party, how about a bottle of the Charles Gardet 1999? This is an exotic fizz with spicy hints of tangerines, sultanas and nuts and is almost a meal in itself. For a much richer and full-bodied wine that is equally remarkable, I'd recommend the Duval-Leroy Blanc de Chardonnay 1998 for its enticing white chocolate flavour and toffee-like aftertaste. This wine is delicious served both on its own or with richly-flavoured dishes.

At a recent retirement party I tasted Bollinger La Grande Année 1997. An impressive fizz with intense creamy and hazelnut overtones, this seems appropriate for a send off and certainly worth retiring for! If a year has a special meaning for you, the year you fell in love, got a great job, achieved a lifelong ambition, then Vintage Champagne is the answer. Among my favourites are Veuve Clicquot Rosé 1999, a moreish fizz with an unusual minty aroma and luscious tangy flavour of *fraise de bois* and Louis Roederer 1999, a multi-layered elegant wine with hints of hazelnuts and a delicate after taste of *fraise de bois*. These are fizzes that make you want to rejoice just on tasting them!

For more birthday and anniversary fizz suggestions, see page 72

new year's eve

Everyone drinks fizz on New Year's Eve and if you prefer to have a small, select dinner party, it's the perfect time for vintage Champagne. If you are lucky enough to get your hands on some legendary Krug 1990, then I would recommend sharing it only with very close friends and those you know are serious fizz fans. This wine is class in a glass with hints of spicy apricots and hazelnuts and a lively mousse. Krug's single vineyard vintage wine Clos du Mesnil 1979 remains the most complex vintage Champagne I have ever been privileged enough to enjoy. I saw the new millennium in with a cherished bottle of the 1979 vintage – a wine as heady as the moment itself. I can recall the richness of the fruit flavour and the exotic, lingering aftertaste. I'm glad to report that the 1995 vintage has all the hallmarks of a really great wine too with a mind-blowingly

intense, multi-layered fruit and floral aftertaste. This wine can be laid down and kept for some time. More affordable is the Deutz 1998, a rich wine with toasted fruit and a flavour that's reminiscent of bread and butter pudding. If you prefer a lighter, more zippy fizz then Joseph Perrier 1998 is the fizz to search out. It's tangy, mouth-wateringly juicy raspberry flavour makes it extremely moreish. I've been a great fan of the wines from the house of Taittinger all my professional life and their skill is ever more evident in their deluxe cuvée. The Taittinger Comtes de Champagne Rosé 1999 is a stunning wine with a rich

nectarines and cream flavour – I can think of no more delightful and memorable way of seeing in the new year.
For more party fizz suggestions see pages 10, 41, 61, 71 and 85

wedding toasts

Normally you only get one glass for a toast, so you need to make sure it is something really special! At the toast at my own wedding we drank Heidsieck Monopole Diamant Bleu 1961, a present from my father. It was produced the year I was born and guests were enchanted to be drinking a wine with as much bottle age as the

bride! Even 20 years on I can still recall that intense creamy toasted flavour. The only other wine I have tasted from this vintage was a magnum of Lanson 1961. It was incredibly youthful with lively, stylish, crisp fruit and a lingering, tangy aftertaste. Veuve Clicquot's Rich 1999 is the perfect complement to wedding cake and is a great favourite. This is a fizz that is halfway between brut and demi-sec in terms of sweetness and is very moreish. Rich with honeycomb and toffee-like fruit, this has a spicy sweetness on the finish, balanced by tangy lime-like acidity. Some people choose to mark the toast with a

rosé. Try Gosset's aptly named Celebris 1998, which is an impressive fizz with tangy redcurrant-like overtones. Its stunning orangey-pink colour and fine mousse will make even the most rowdy guests sit up and take notice! Pol Roger continues to go from strength to strength and I think if I ever got married again, I would choose to serve a fizz from this house. The 1998 Rosé is no exception with its elegant, pale salmon-pink colour and its enticing red fruit aroma. It reminds me of sunshine and summer pudding!

For more wedding fizz suggestions, see pages 10, 51, 65 and 72

dining in style

This is about decadence. Whether I'm holding a candle-lit dinner at home or dining out, fabulous fizz has to be on the menu. Part of the charm of fizz is that you can enjoy it throughout the meal. It's not just for aperitifs. And going the fizz route saves pondering on the red or white question. Vintage Champagnes veer towards the richer, more full-bodied style and therefore these wines are particularly suitable to drink with food. Veuve Clicquot's La Grande Dame Rosé 1995 is one of the most stunning wines I have ever tasted. It is named after the legendary

Champagne's for women.
I stick to claret.

Clive Newcome from *The Newcomers*, by W. M. Thackeray

Madame Clicquot, an astute business woman who put Champagne on the map throughout the world. This wine is a fitting tribute to her – open a bottle and its aroma fills the room. Salmon pink in colour with a delicate, fine mousse, it has an intense aroma and flavour that literally leaps out of the glass with delicious raspberry ripple fruit and a tangy acidity that cuts through the ice cream-like finish. It's very moreish and with every sip, a new flavour or nuance is detected. While a meal in itself, this wine sings out when served with roast English lamb or baked salmon. Roast pork also goes well with vintage Champagne. Pol Roger 1998 is a mind-blowing wine, laiden with rich appley flavour – ideal with both crisp crackling and apple sauce as well as apple crumble or tart. Henriot 1996 is also a good contender with complex juicy fruit and a hint of baked apples on the finish. Seafood, especially crab calls for a substantial full-bodied wine. Gosset Grand Millesime 1999 is ideal as its rich, honeycomb-like fruit flavour accentuates the sweetness in the crab, yet cuts through the richness of dishes like crab bisque. With scallops enjoy the creamy, tangy richness of Besserat de Bellefon 1998 or the clean cut red fruit flavour of Duval-Leroy 1996 with its hint of violet-like fruit.

For more dinner-party fizz suggestions, see pages 63 and 76

christmas

Christmas Eve, for me, is often more of a special occasion than Christmas Day itself. I think it's the anticipation of the fun ahead. One of my fondest memories of a particular Christmas Eve revolves around a magnum of Champagne Veuve Clicquot La Grande Dame 1985, the perfect complement to grilled lobster and Jersey potatoes. Steely yet elegant with amazing balance, this is one of the finest Champagnes I have ever tasted. Great wines need to be shared with other people. I enjoyed this with a best friend and we found the magnum to be just the right size. What hedonistic days! Sadly I've not come across any magnums of this fine wine since, but I am glad to report that the bottle of Veuve Clicquot La Grande Dame 1996 I tasted more recently confirmed my view that this is one of the very best deluxe cuvées around. Rich with a toasted, almost meaty aroma this has rich, oily, buttery fruit with a passion-fruit-like touch of refreshing acidity on the finish. On Christmas Day

morning, Vintage Champagne is a luxury over a leisurely breakfast. It's also the perfect drink to quench your thirst when opening presents! Nicolas Feuillatte 1999 is the perfect sharpener, with its moreish and easy-drinking floral fruit flavour and sherbet-like aftertaste. Taittinger 1999 is a very good bet too, especially if you are having kedgeree or kippers for breakfast. It's creamy flavour, with buttery richness, makes for a great start to the day. And if supplies permit, this will taste good with turkey or goose too. I'm a great believer in serving Champagne throughout the meal, especially as it saves on the washing up! So with lunch, how about a glass of the stunning Louis Roederer 1999 Rosé, with

its lusciously perfumed strawberry aroma and passionfruit tang on the finish. Charles Gardet 2001 tastes great with turkey; this creamy, strawberry-like fizz has an appropriate touch of cranberry zippiness on the finish. Billecart-Salmon is a favourite Champagne house of mine. Their Cuvée Nicolas François Billecart 1996 is a real stunner with blowsy, honeyed fruit and a toffee aftertaste: it's the perfect foil for turkey or guinea fowl. While it might sound like word association, the Canard-Duchêne 2000, with its rich and intense apple aroma and sherbet-like fruit, really does taste brilliant with duck! When all the excitement of the day has passed and the children have finally gone to bed, why not

treat yourself to a glass of the stylish Jacquesson, Avize Grand Cru 1996. This has an aroma like brioche and a moreish mango and cream flavour. Or, instead of hot chocolate, how about a glass of Nicolas Feuillatte Grand Cru 1996? A sublime white chocolate flavour with an aftertaste of raspberries. But the ultimate way to end a perfect day is with a glass of the legendary Dom Pérignon 1998 from Moët & Chandon, with its elegant, rose petal aroma and deliciously creamy hazelnut luscious fruit this is the stuff of dreams...

For more Christmas fizz suggestions, see pages 101 and 104

Please note – the vintages specified in this section were current at the time of writing.

One of my fondest memories of Christmas Eve revolves around a magnum of Veuve Clicquot La Grande Dame 1985 and grilled lobster. Steely, yet elegant, with amazing balance, this is one of the finest Champagnes I've ever tasted.

IS THAT CHAMPAGNE?
THEN PUT IT DOWN THE DRAIN!
IT'S BOGUS AND IT'S BILIOUS,
IT'S A BANE.
FORTY BOB A BOTTLE! WELL,
IT MAY AMUSE A PEER;
SOME WOULD TAKE TO WATER IF
THE PRICE OF IT WAS DEAR,
BUT WHO'D BUY A BUBBLY IF IT
COST THE SAME AS BEER?
STILL, IF THAT'S CHAMPAGNE
YOU CAN FILL MY GLASS AGAIN.

A. P. Herbert, *Ballads for Broadbrows*

taste notes
A quick reference guide to the best Vintage Champagnes

Vintage Rosé Champagne

Charles Gardet 2001 *'Easy drinking, intense rosé with strawberries and cream flavour'*

Deutz 2000 *'Delicately coloured rosé with intensely aromatic overtones of rhubarb and a strawberry sherbet finish'*

Jacquart 2000 *'Orangey pink, full-bodied fizz with honeyed, rich, rounded caramel flavour'*

Louis Roederer 1999 *'Sophisticated fizz with luscious, perfumed strawberries and cream-like flavour'*

Moët & Chandon 1999 *'Unusual aroma of violets and hazlenuts with cream flavour'*

Perrier-Jouët Belle Epoque 1999 *'Orangey pink aperitif-style fizz with hints of strawberry jam'*

Tattinger Comtes de Champagne 1999 *'Rich, stylish nectarines and cream-like fizz with lingering aftertaste'*

Veuve Clicquot Rosé 1999 *'Intense, full-bodied rose with minty aroma and flavour of forest fruits'*

Gosset Celebris 1998 *'Pale orange classy aperitif-style fizz with tangy, floral overtones'*

Pol Roget 1998 *'Intense salmon pink with enticing red fruit aroma and flavour – just like summer pudding'*

Billecart-Salmon 1996 *'Classy, moreish fizz with mouth-watering summer pudding and cream flavour'*

Charles Heidsieck Cuvée 1996 *'Rich, intense, full-bodied fizz with hint of pears and red berry compote'*

Veuve Clicquot La Grande Dame 1995 *'Intense, complex wine with layers of raspberry ripple flavour'*

Vintage Champagne

Canard-Duchêne 2000 *'Rich with intense appley flavour and sherbet-like creamy finish'*

Duval-Leroy Authentis, Cumières 2000 *'Unusual minty, floral fizz with a hint of sweetness'*

Nicholas Feuillatte 2000 *'Luscious, slightly sweet fizz with moreish flavour of honeycomb and poached pears'*

Duval-Leroy, Authentis, Trépail 1999 *'Intense rich creamy fizz with long-lingering aftertaste'*

Gosset Grand Millésime 1999 *'Rich, honeycomb-like wine with intense multi-layered fruit flavour'*

Nicholas Feuillatte 1999 *'Easy-drinking, floral fizz with tangy sherbet-like fruit'*

Tattinger 1999 *'Full-bodied, with classy, intense yeasty creamy aroma and flavour'*

Canard-Duchêne 1999 *'Easy drinking apple sorbet-like fizz'*

Moët & Chandon 1999 *'Honeyed with apple and pear overtones and rich, slightly sweet finish'*

Veuve Clicquot Rich 1999 *'A rich honeycomb and toffee aroma with a creamy sweetness'*

Cuvée Charles Gardet 1999 *'Exotic fizz with spicy hints of tangerines, sultanas and nuts'*

Louis Roederer 1999 *'Stylish and multi-layered with hints of hazlenuts and forest fruits'*

Besserat de Bellefon 1998 *'Intense, pear-like aroma with stylish, creamy yet tangy finish'*

Deutz 1998 *'Rich with toasted, creamy aroma reminiscent of bread and butter pudding'*

Jacquart Cuvée Mosaique 1998 *'Moreish, raspberry ripple-like fizz'*

Joseph Perrier 1998 *'Tangy, juicy fruit with mouth-watering raspberry flavours'*

Moët & Chandon Dom Pérignon 1998 *'Elegant, complex fizz with hints of rose petals and hazelnut overtones'*

Perrier-Jouët 1998 *'Yeasty aromas with a hint of cherries'*

Pol Roger 1998 *'Intense, mind-blowing wine with mouth-watering apples and cream flavours'*

Heidsieck Gold Top 1997 *'Rich, buttery, golden fizz with creamy, pear-like aftertaste'*

Alfred Gratien 1997 *'Aperitif, dry-style with elegant, tangy sherbet-like fruit'*

Lanson Noble Cuvée 1997 *'Intense fizz with butterscotch and pineapple nuances'*

Bollinger La Grande Année 1997 *'Creamy wine with hazlenut nuances'*

Billecart-Salmon Cuvée Nicolas François Billecart 1996 *'Rich and blousey with honeyed toffee and fruit flavour'*

Bruno Paillard 1996 *'Rich, creamy, yeasty fizz with hints of liquorice and tangy red fruits'*

Duval-Leroy 1996 *'Mouthwatering, red tangy fruit flavour with hints of violets'*

Henriot 1996 *'Full-bodied, honeycomb fizz with baked apple nuances'*

Jacquesson, Avize Grand Cru 1996 *'Unusual, floral aroma with intense flavour of brioche and creamy mangoes'*

Lanson 1996 *'Butterscotch, rich, full-bodied wine with baked apples aftertaste'*

Laurent-Perrier 1996 *'Stylish with honeycomb and dried apricot tones'*

Nicolas Feuillatte Grand Cru 1996 *'Exotic white chocolate-like tangy fruit'*

Perrier-Jouët Belle Epoque 1996 *'Rounded, sweetish fizz with hints of apricots and cream'*

Piper Heidsieck 1996 *'Full-bodied buttery wine with moreish red fruit flavour'*

Tattinger Comtes de Champagne, Blanc de Blancs 1996 *'Rich and elegant, with perfumed red fruit'*

Veuve Clicquot La Grande Dame 1996 *'Rich, with toasted aroma and creamy, buttery overtones'*

Joseph Perrier, Cuvée Josephine 1995 *'Stylish with multi-layered fruit flavour and creamy pear finish'*

Jacquesson Grand Vin Signature 1995 *'Stylish, dry, aperitif fizz with nutty overtones'*

Krug Clos du Mésnil 1995 *'Mind-blowing, floral and creamy multi-layered fizz'*

Mumm 1995 *'Easy drinking, rich, full-bodied honeycomb-like fizz'*

Pol Roget Cuvée Sir Winston Churchill 1995 *'Rich, luscious wine with apricots and ginger'*

Krug 1990 *'Complex, full-bodied fizz with hints of hazlenuts and spicy apricots'*

demi-sec bubblies

Softly fruity demi-sec fizzes, with a subtle balance of sweetness and refreshing, tangy acidity.

i n the early part of the 20th century demi-sec Champagne was *the* society fizz. All the right people drank it; and it certainly kept the 1920s 'roaring'. Now with the start of a new century, it seems this style of sweeter fizz is enjoying something of a cult revival, which I think is brilliant, as there are some really exciting, seductive sweet sparkling wines around. Start looking and you will quickly uncover these gently sweet bubblies (look out for the term 'demi-sec' or occasionally *riche*) in the shops and on restaurant wine lists.

As you'll discover, 'sweet' doesn't necessarily mean heavy, or sugary. The great thing about good-quality demi-sec fizz is that it has a subtle balance of sweetness and refreshing, tangy acidity. It is this 'backbone' of acid – a crisp, sherbet-like, tangy taste on the finish – that stops the fizz from tasting cloyingly sweet. On a sweetness scale of 1–9, where 1 indicates a bone-dry wine and 9 a very rich, sticky sweet one, most demi-sec sparkling wines tend to weigh in at around 6. The popular, gently sweet Italian sparkler Asti Spumante (see page 103), for example, averages 7.

Some people say this style of fizz is an acquired taste. What is closer to the truth is that many may simply not have tasted a good quality demi-sec fizz with the finesse and style of those you'll find here. And they've no doubt not drunk it in the company of the most flattering dishes, because, as with many of the richer fizzes in this book, sweet fizz undoubtedly tastes at its best with food. With puddings it is superb – fruit-based ice creams and sorbets are beautifully complemented by demi-sec fizz.

So dare to be different, join the cult and offer your guests a glass of gently sweet fizz with their dessert. Just don't be surprised if they ask for a second glass to enjoy on its own afterwards. If you know your friends will enjoy the fun of experimenting with unusual combinations, take a look at the fizzes I've suggested here to serve with savoury dishes; you'll be amazed at the stunning combinations they can make. And they're guaranteed to get everyone talking.

puddings

I defy anyone who 'thinks' they won't enjoy a sweet fizz not to be seduced by Champagne Louis Roederer Riche NV. The current non-vintage has an intense toasted, caramelly aroma with a hint of almonds on the palate. While rich, it is not very sweet at all, with just an attractive touch of honey before the refreshing zip of acidity on the finish. Recently I served some half-bottles of aged Louis Roederer Riche (you could tell they were old from the indented corks and the deep colour of the wine). They were absolute nectar and slipped down beautifully with the tutti-frutti Champagne sorbet that I served, which had crunchy bits of raspberry in it.

Fruit-based puddings and sweet fizzes are really made for each other. You can enjoy a glass of demi-sec with anything from an apple crumble, a tarte Tatin or caramelised oranges to summer pudding and strawberry Pavlova. Champagne Pol Roger Demi-Sec NV, with its creamy apple-like flavour, tastes amazing with apple pie and cream or baked apples filled with sultanas and cinnamon. Lots of other puddings make for perfect demi-sec partners too. Try serving an old favourite such as bread and butter pudding with a glass of Champagne Canard-Duchêne Demi-Sec NV, which has an

'A life of pleasure-seeking, card playing and dissipation brings only dissatisfaction. You will find that one day.'
'Oh I know it turns out that way sometimes,' assented Reginald. 'Forbidden fizz is often the sweetest.'
But the remark was wasted on the princess, who preferred Champagne that had at least a suggestion of dissolved barley-sugar.

Saki, *Reginald in Russia*

Fruit-based puddings and sweet fizzes are really made for each other. You can enjoy a glass of demi-sec with anything from an apple crumble, a tarte Tatin or caramelised oranges to summer pudding and Pavlova.

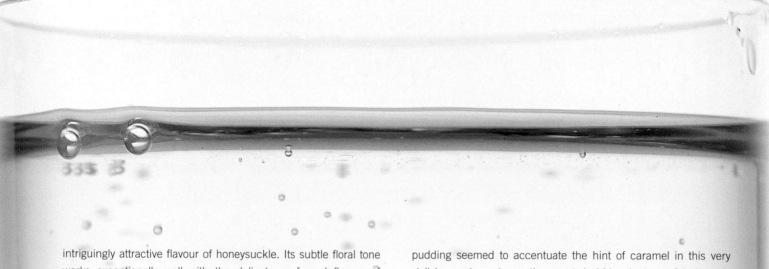

intriguingly attractive flavour of honeysuckle. Its subtle floral tone works exceptionally well with the delicate perfumed flavour of Champagne and Rose-Petal Sorbet (see page 120). I've also enjoyed this fizz with butterscotch ice cream, the flavour of which can sometimes be flattened by still sweet wines.

If you want to win over the most doubting of friends, give them a glass of a refreshingly light, elegant demi-sec fizz such as the sweetly fruity Bouvet Saumur Demi-Sec. With its characteristic honeyed Chenin Blanc character and gently spritzy character, this is a lovely summery style of sweet fizz.

Sadly, chocolate is a bit of a problem. Rich chocolate mousse, for example, can swamp the fizz. However, for those of you who simply love chocolate, I have found a solution or two. A glass of sweet fizz such as the Champagne Piper Heidsieck Demi-Sec NV, with its creamy sherbet flavours and floral finish, will complement a light chocolate dessert. Asti Spumante can withstand a limited chocolate onslaught, too. Or you can be really daring and pour a sparkling red wine (see page 104).

Asti Spumante is a star choice to serve with Christmas pudding, by the way. As light and gently sweet as the pudding can be dark and heavy, this soft, spritzy Italian fizz really revives the taste buds! (See page 103 for top producers.) While there are not yet that many sweet sparklers made outside Europe, one well worth searching out is the Australian Green Point Riche NV. I recently tasted it with a dish of grilled figs served with sour cream and orange caramel. It was a fabulous combination. The caramel in the pudding seemed to accentuate the hint of caramel in this very stylish, again not overtly sweet bubbly. Just as fabulous is Schramsberg Napa Valley Crémant 1995. This is a very easy to drink sweet fizz, with a delicious raspberry-ripple-like flavour.

Trendy puddings such as sticky toffee pudding or pecan pie taste good with demi-sec too. For a relaxed Friday evening supper, why not indulge in the grapey Asti Spumante or a demi-sec cava from Spain, two really affordable sweet fizzes? One of the nicest cavas that I have recently enjoyed is Rondel Premier Cuvée Demi-Sec NV. It is floral and sweet, yet superbly balanced. Strangely enough, it tastes great with spicy, Asian dishes too....
For more pudding fizz suggestions, see page 88

savoury dishes

Believe it or not, demi-sec fizz can be sensational with savoury dishes too. For an unusual, yet very successful pairing, serve it with lobster bisque or fish pâté as a first course. It's quite amazing how that touch of sweetness in the wine allows it to stand up to powerful food flavours. This style of fizz is also a good foil for duck, especially in Chinese dishes such as crispy Peking duck, where the sweetness complements the richness of the plum sauce. Prawns or fish served with garlic and chilli, or cooked Thai-style with lemongrass also taste especially good with an accompanying glass of demi-sec. Go on, be adventurous, try any of these savoury dishes with one of the recommended demi-sec fizzes on pages 102–103.

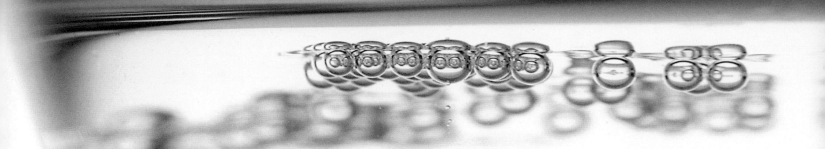

taste notes

A quick reference guide to the best demi-sec fizzes

France – Champagne

Canard-Duchêne Demi-Sec NV *'Pale gold with honeysuckle sweetness'*

Louis Roederer Riche NV *'Toasted caramel, almondy aroma and flavour'*

Piper Heidsieck Demi-Sec NV *'Creamy, floral, sherbet flavours'*

Pol Roger Demi-Sec NV *'Apples and cream with sherbet on the finish'*

France – Loire

Bouvet Saumur Demi-Sec *'Fresh and elegant, gently honeyed fizz'*

Spain – Cava

Rondel Premier Cuvée Demi-Sec NV *'Floral, spicy, sweet fizz'*

Australia

Green Point Riche NV *'Stylish, with hints of caramel and citrus acidity on the finish'*

California

Schramsberg Napa Valley Crémant 1995 *'More-ish, with a delicious raspberry-ripple flavour'*

Italy – Asti

Asti Spumante – *top producers include Asti Martini, Fontanafredda and Bruno Giacosa*

Moscato d'Asti – *top producers include Marco Negri, Alasia, La Morandina, La Spinetta,*

Saracco Paolo, Vignaioli di Santo Stefano Belbo

wicked and red

Full-flavoured, rich and sweetly fruity red fizzes, with a dry, slightly tannic finish

If you are searching for a really original style of bubbly that will make your friends sit up and take notice, why not try a spectacular red fizz? These are serious but fun sparkling wines. An acquired taste, yes, but if you like them, you'll love them. Just watch people's faces as the cork pops and all that frothing purple fizz comes pouring out. Made from the spicy, plummy Shiraz grape, Australia produces a unique style of fabulous red fizz that is now spreading its influence around the globe. While there aren't yet that many widely available, these unusual fizzes are well worth seeking out.

Probably the most fabulous I have tasted to date is Mitchell's extremely full-bodied tannic Peppertree Sparkling Shiraz NV. Richly spicy in aroma and flavour, with a hint of black pepper, this is a classic Aussie sparkling red and a great introduction to the style. An indulgent option is the Seppelt Show Sparkling Shiraz. A vintage-dated fizz, this is allowed to mature for over eight years before release, and is much sweeter, softer and more approachable because of that bottle age. Its younger brother, Sparkling Shiraz from Seppelt has an amazing black-cherry aroma and earthy plain-chocolate flavours. Australia also makes red fizz from the Cabernet Sauvignon grape. Yalumba Cuvée Two Sparkling Cabernet NV has a wonderful aroma of black-currants with a hint of cinnamon spice.

Believe it or not, red fizz is fabulous with food, both savoury and sweet. Chilled Sparkling Shiraz is a traditional accompaniment to Christmas turkey and cranberry sauce Down Under. It also works wonders with Indian dishes or choose a red fizz with dark red fruit and chocolate characters for a wickedly good partner to chocolate torte. Try the Yalumba Cuvée Two with a good blue cheese such as English Stilton.

California now boasts some stunning red fizzes made from the seductive Pinot Noir grape variety. And as I discovered on a recent trip to the USA, they are quite extraordinarily good served with red meats, such as roast lamb or beef. Korbel Rouge NV is a full-bodied red fizz, with an unusual liquorice flavour. Schug Rouge de Noir 1996 positively brims with intense strawberry-jam fruit.

A quick reference guide to the best red fizzes

Australia

Peppertree Sparkling Shiraz NV, Mitchell *'Intense, spicy, with hints of black pepper'*

Seppelt Sparkling Shiraz 1994 *'Black-cherry with plain chocolate flavours'*

Yalumba Cuvée Two Sparkling Cabernet NV *'Blackcurrants and cinnamon-like spice'*

California

Korbel Rouge NV *'Full-bodied, spicy, liquorice-like red fizz'*

Schug Rouge de Noir 1996 *'Mouth-watering, strawberry-jam fruit'*

Mumm Sparkling Pinot Noir NV *'Delicious aroma and flavour of fraise des bois'*

Kornell Rouge NV *'Floral overtones, with raspberry-ripple-like finish'*

Just watch people's faces as the cork pops and all that frothing purple fizz comes pouring out.

fizz cocktails and recipes

The secret to making successful cocktails at home is to keep them simple. And with fabulous fizz as the main magic ingredient, they are bound to taste good! The million-dollar question is, of course, what sort of fizz should you use? Personally, I think it is a mistake to use vintage, deluxe champagne or the very best, most expensive sparkling wines. Instead I prefer a light- to medium-bodied, everyday kind of fizz, such as the affordable and great-quality Australian Angus Brut NV, the consistently good Californian fizz Mumm Cuvée Napa NV or Spanish cava, or for something slightly more fruity, a French sparkler such as Blanquette de Limoux. If you want much sweeter cocktails, use a sweet demi-sec fizz or a sweet Italian fizz such as Asti Spumante or Moscato d'Asti.

In terms of quantities, to avoid measuring out ingredients, simply keep to the proportions stated and gauge the measure by eye. This means you can make as much or as little as you wish, irrespective of the size of the glass or jug. When making fruit-based cocktails, always use freshly squeezed fruit juice for a more refreshing taste.

Finally, as ever with fabulous fizz, make sure it's well chilled and don't be tempted to make cocktails in advance or you will reduce the all-important bubble-count.

cocktails

bellini

*A classic cocktail that originated in Venice
and traditionally is made with puréed white
peaches. It's simple but very more-ish,
and one glass inevitably leads to another.*

3–4 ripe peaches, skinned, stones
   removed and flesh cut into chunks
peach brandy (optional)
1 bottle brut fizz

In a blender, whizz the peaches to a
purée, then chill. Fill 6–8 Champagne
flutes one-third full of purée, dash with
brandy, if using, and top with chilled fizz.

buck's fizz

*Perfect as a toast at a breakfast reception
or served as an aperitif. Created by the
bartender at Buck's Club, London, in 1921.*

1 part freshly squeezed orange juice
Grenadine (optional)
2 parts brut fizz
1 slice of orange (optional)

Pour the orange juice into a Champagne
flute, dash with Grenadine, if using, and
top up with chilled fizz. Add a slice of
orange, if using, then serve.

kir royale

*Stylish and delicious, with a rich
blackcurrant flavour. Vary the liqueur to
create another cocktail – use crème de
framboise, made from raspberries, or
crème de mûres, made from blackberries.*

crème de cassis, to taste
1 part brut fizz

Put a few drops, about ½ teaspoon, of
crème de cassis into a Champagne flute,
top up with chilled fizz and stir to mix.

champagne julep

*Excellent for summertime entertaining –
outside in the open air or under cover in a
marquee. It's suitably light and refreshing.*

1 sugar cube
1 part brut fizz
1 sprig of fresh mint

Put a sugar cube into a Champagne flute
or saucer glass and top up with chilled
sparkling wine. Add a sprig of fresh mint
to the glass, then serve.

champagne pick-me-up

The title says it all! Why not enjoy this cocktail while relaxing in a hot bath?

1 part brandy
1 part dry white vermouth, sweet white
   vermouth or sweet red vermouth
caster sugar, to taste
4 parts brut fizz

Put the brandy, vermouth and sugar in a Champagne flute or saucer glass. Top up with chilled sparkling wine.

blue rinse fizz

A heavenly cocktail – electric-blue in colour – with a tropical feel.

4 dashes or 1 teaspoon blue Curaçao
1 part brut fizz
1 slice of orange

Chill a Champagne flute in the freezer for 1 hour. Add the Curaçao and swirl it around the glass to coat the inside. Add the fizz and serve with a slice of orange.

champagne st clements

Refreshingly tangy, the bitter-sweet flavour of the Cointreau and lime makes this fizzy cocktail mouth-wateringly good.

1 part freshly squeezed lemon or lime
   juice
1 part Cointreau
4 parts brut fizz
1 slice of orange, lemon or lime

Mix the lemon or lime juice and Cointreau with some crushed ice, then pour into a tall glass to about one-third full. Top up with chilled sparkling wine and serve with a slice of orange, lemon or lime.

black velvet

Sex in a glass – rich in body with silky smooth bubbles. Created in 1861 at Brook's Club, London. For a match made in heaven, serve this cocktail with oysters – an acclaimed aphrodisiac.

1 part brut fizz
1 part draught stout such as Guinness
   or Murphy's (draught stout is available
   in cans)

Chill the fizz and stout, then pour them simultaneously into a tall glass. To create a very frothy head on the cocktail, add a dash more fizz. For a sweeter cocktail, use Murphy's instead of Guinness.

champagne cocktail

An extremely chic aperitif. The effervescent bubbles spiralling their way to the top as the sugar dissolves is quite hypnotic.

1 sugar cube
dash of Angostura bitters
1 teaspoon brandy or Cognac
1 part brut fizz

Put a sugar cube into a Champagne saucer glass and dash with Angostura to soak. Add the brandy and top with fizz.

calypso fizz

One taste will transport you to the exotic shores of the Caribbean!

1 part white rum or coconut rum
1 part banana or orange liqueur, such as Cointreau
dash of Angostura bitters (optional)
4 parts brut fizz
1 slice of banana
1 slice of orange

Put some crushed ice into a Champagne saucer glass. Add the rum and the banana or orange liqueur and dash with Angostura bitters, if using. Top up with fizz and stir gently to mix. Serve with a slice of banana and a twist of orange.

death in the afternoon

Said to be one of Ernest Hemingway's favourites when he lived in Paris.

1 part Pernod
5 parts brut fizz

Pour the Pernod into a Champagne flute and add the chilled sparkling wine to give a milky opalescent cocktail.

mexican sunrise

Unusual bitter-sweet flavour. Gold tequila is a must – it is richer, smoother and sweeter than standard tequila.

4 parts brut fizz
1 part gold tequila
1 part freshly squeezed lemon juice
1 teaspoon clear honey (optional)

Put the chilled fizz, gold tequila and lemon juice in a tall glass, then stir in the honey, if using. Serve with a straw.

alfonso fizz

Desposed in 1931, Spanish King Alfonso XIII bid a hasty retreat to France, where he made his time bearable with this drink.

1 sugar cube
3 drops Angostura bitters
1 part Dubonnet
4 parts brut fizz
1 slice of lemon

Put the sugar cube in a Champagne flute or saucer glass and add the Angostura. Add a large ice cube, the Dubonnet and chilled fizz. Serve with a twist of lemon.

champagne charlie

Named after the infamous Charles Heidsieck – this is a true party drink.

4 parts Charles Heidsieck NV
1 part apricot brandy
1 slice of orange

Half fill a glass with crushed ice. Add the fizz and brandy. Serve with the orange slice.

champagne fruit punch

Make at the last minute or you will lose the fabulous fizz. If unexpected guests arrive, simply add more fizz or sparkling mineral water to replenish the punch.

2 parts sparkling wine, such as Asti
    Spumante or Moscato d'Asti
1 part sparkling mineral water
½ part brandy
⅛ part cherry brandy
freshly squeezed lemon juice, to taste
caster sugar, to taste
a selection of fruit, such as peach slices,
    cherries, raspberries, orange slices,
    pineapple chunks, starfruit slices and
    kiwi slices.
sprigs of fresh mint, to serve

Put all the ingredients, except the fruit, in a punch bowl or large glass bowl and stir to mix. Add the fruit and mint and serve in tall glasses or Champagne flutes.

champagne float

An alcoholic version of the all-time-favourite, ice cream soda.

1 large scoop vanilla ice cream
1 tablespoon cherry brandy
dash of Cointreau (optional)
1 part brut fizz
raspberries, to serve

Put the ice cream in a tall glass. Add the cherry brandy and Cointreau, if using, and top with chilled sparkling wine. Stir gently to mix, then add the raspberries. Serve with a straw and soda spoon.

fizzy applejack

A treat for lovers of apple brandy.

1 part Calvados
dash of Grenadine
4 parts brut fizz
1 slice of apple

Pour the Calvados, Grenadine and fizz into a glass and serve with a slice of apple.

cherry froth

Seriously potent. You've been warned!

1 part vodka
1 part cherry brandy
dash of freshly squeezed lime juice
2 parts brut fizz
1 fresh cherry

Pour the vodka, brandy and lime juice into a tall, long-stemmed glass. Top with chilled fizz and serve with a cherry.

the holy grail

Christened appropriately – Benedictine and Champagne are both thought to have been invented by monks.

4 parts brut fizz
1 part brandy
1 part Benedictine
1 part Cointreau
peach or nectarine slices, to taste
1 sprig of fresh rosemary

Mix the first 4 ingredients together, add the fruit and serve with a sprig of rosemary.

carribean cruiser

Have a few of these and you'll be floating!

1 part freshly squeezed orange juice
1 part golden rum
dash of lemon juice
3 parts brut fizz
1 sugar cube (optional)

Put the orange juice, golden rum and lemon juice in a Champagne flute and top with chilled fizz. Drop in the sugar cube, if using, then serve.

texas fizz

Take your time over this intoxicating cocktail. If it proves too powerful, replace half of the fizz with tonic water.

1 part gin
2 parts freshly squeezed orange juice
dash of Grenadine
4 parts brut fizz
1 slice of orange

Put some ice into a large tumbler, then add the gin, orange juice and Grenadine. Top up with chilled fizz and serve with a twist of orange.

melon bubble

Quite a lethal concoction!

2 parts gin
1 part Midori (melon liqueur)
1 part Poire William
4 parts dry brut fizz (if you prefer
   something sweet and grapey, use
   Asti Spumante)
melon balls or pear slices, to serve

Half fill a Champagne flute or saucer
glass with the gin, Midori and Poire
William. Top up with chilled fizz and
serve with melon balls or pear slices.

citrus toast

A mouth-tingling, refreshing fizz – use it
for the toast at any celebration.

1 sugar cube
1 part Grand Marnier
1 part freshly squeezed lime juice
2 parts freshly squeezed orange juice
2 parts brut fizz
slices of lime or small oranges, to serve

Put the sugar cube in the bottom of a
Champagne flute or saucer glass. Add
the remaining ingredients and serve with
slices of lime or orange.

cooking with fizz

Marvellous to drink and wonderful to cook with – fizz imparts a subtle, light flavour that complements fish and seafood, chicken, wild mushrooms and delicate fruits such as peaches, cherries and most berries. Don't use expensive bubblies; instead opt for a value-for-money fizz such as a Spanish cava, Australian fizzes like Angus Brut NV or Seaview NV, New Zealand Lindauer Brut NV or the Californian brut fizz, Mumm Cuvée Napa NV.

champagne prawns

Fizz enhances the delicate flavour of seafood perfectly. A wonderful dinner-party starter or a special light-lunch treat.

50 g unsalted butter

12 small shallots, halved

36 large uncooked prawns, shelled and deveined, tail fins left on

2 tablespoons brandy, warmed

250 ml fizz, such as New Zealand Lindauer Brut NV

250 ml crème fraîche

sea salt and freshly ground black pepper

sprigs of fresh dill or chervil, to serve

Italian ciabatta bread, to serve

Serves 6 as a starter or 3 as a main course

Heat the butter in a wide frying pan, add the shallots and sauté gently until softened but not browned, about 3–5 minutes. Add the prawns and cook until opaque – about 3 minutes, but no longer or they will be tough. Remove the prawns and shallots with a slotted spoon and reserve. Pour the warmed brandy into the pan, light with a match and let the alcohol burn off. Add the fizz and bring to the boil, then reduce the heat and simmer until the liquid has reduced by half. Stir in the crème fraîche and add the salt and freshly ground black pepper. Cook the sauce for 2 minutes, then reduce the heat and return the prawns and shallots to the pan to heat through. Serve with sprigs of fresh dill or chervil and crusty bread, such as ciabatta to mop up the juices.

champagne chicken

Succulent and tender with a subtle tang and richness from the fizz. Elegant simplicity is the key to this superb dish.

2 tablespoons butter
1 teaspoon peanut or corn oil
6 slices pancetta or 4 slices smoked streaky bacon, cut into strips
1 chicken, cut into 8 pieces
¼ bottle brut fizz, such as Mumm Cuvée Napa NV
2 sprigs of fresh tarragon, chopped, plus extra to serve
sea salt and freshly ground black pepper

Serves 6-8

Heat the butter and oil in a large frying pan. Add the pancetta or bacon and fry until crispy, then remove and drain on kitchen paper. Add the chicken pieces to the pan and cook for 5 minutes on each side until golden. Pour in the fizz, bring to the boil and let bubble for 1–2 minutes, then add the pancetta or bacon and tarragon. Bring to the boil, cover and reduce the heat to a gentle simmer. Cook the chicken until tender, about 50 minutes, basting 2–3 times during cooking. (If the sauce reduces too much, add a few tablespoons of water) Serve with sprigs of tarragon, boiled new potatoes and sautéed mushrooms.

wild mushroom and champagne risotto

A remarkable risotto. For best results, use the finest and freshest ingredients, and whatever wild mushrooms are in season.

10 g dried porcini mushrooms
300 g assorted fresh wild mushrooms, such as oyster, chanterelle, morel and shiitake, or button mushrooms

75 g unsalted butter
1 tablespoon olive oil
1 onion, finely chopped
1 garlic clove, crushed
500 g Arborio risotto rice
1 large glass fizz, such as Angus Brut
1½ litres chicken or vegetable stock, kept simmering
sea salt and freshly ground black pepper
chopped flat leaf parsley, to serve

Serves 4 as a light lunch or 6 as a starter

Put the dried porcini in a small bowl, cover with hot water and let soak for 10 minutes. Strain through a muslin-lined sieve and reserve the soaking liquid, then coarsely chop the porcini. Using a damp cloth, wipe clean the fresh mushrooms and thickly slice any that are large.

Heat 25 g of the butter and the oil in a large saucepan. Add the onion and cook until softened but not browned, about 5 minutes, then add the garlic and cook for 2 minutes more. Add the fresh wild mushrooms, fry gently for 2 minutes, then add the chopped porcini.

Add the rice and stir until the grains are translucent. Pour in the fizz and the reserved soaking liquid and cook over a medium heat until all the liquid has been absorbed. Add a ladleful of hot stock to the pan of rice and cook, stirring until absorbed. Continue to add ladles of hot stock at intervals, allowing each addition to be absorbed before adding more, until the risotto is plump, soft and creamy – about 30 minutes. (You may not need to add all the stock.)

Remove the saucepan from the heat and stir in the remaining butter. Season with salt and freshly ground black pepper, then cover and let stand for 2-3 minutes. Serve sprinkled with chopped parsley.

champagne and rose-petal sorbet

A fabulously fragrant dessert with a subtle hint of rose. Use roses that are naturally scented and have not been sprayed.

Syrup:

250 g caster sugar

225 ml water

6 scented rose heads, washed and petals removed, or 1 tablespoon rosewater

½ bottle of demi-sec Champagne, such as Piper Heidsieck NV

juice of ½ lemon

1 egg white, lightly whisked

Serves 4–6

Put the sugar and water in a small saucepan and stir over a low heat until the sugar dissolves. Add the prepared rose petals and bring the mixture to a gentle boil. Reduce the heat and simmer for 10 minutes until a light syrup forms. Remove from the heat and, using a slotted spoon, remove and discard the rose petals. Let syrup cool. For an intense rose flavour, remove petals after syrup has cooled. If using rosewater, add to the cooled syrup.

In a medium-sized bowl, mix the rose-infused syrup, fizz and lemon juice, then fold in the lightly whisked egg white. Transfer to an ice-cream making machine and churn (according to the manufacturer's instructions) until firm. Alternatively, pour the prepared mixture into flat, freezer trays and part-freeze to a slush. Using a fork, beat the slush to break up ice crystals, then return to the freezer. Repeat, then freeze until firm. To serve, remove from the freezer and soften in the refrigerator for 15 minutes, then scoop the sorbet into small bowls or chilled champagne glasses. Best eaten within 2–3 hours of making.

bubbly baked peaches

Fresh, juicy peaches baked in delicious Champagne are a winning combination. They taste even better the next day when the flavours have fully developed.

4 large, ripe peaches
50 g almond ratafia biscuits, crushed
50 g flaked almonds, lightly toasted and
   roughly chopped
3 tablespoons light brown sugar
25 g unsalted butter, plus extra for
   greasing
150 ml demi-sec Champagne, such as
   Louis Roederer Riche NV
whipping cream, lightly whipped, to serve
Serves 4 or 8

Cut the peaches in half and remove and discard the stones. Using a teaspoon, scoop out some of the flesh from the cavity in the peaches, then coarsely chop the bits. Put the chopped peaches, crushed ratafia biscuits, chopped almonds and sugar in a bowl and mix well.

Put the peach halves in a lightly buttered, shallow baking dish and fill the hollowed-out centres with the almond and peach mixture. Dot the tops with butter and pour the Champagne over.

Bake, uncovered, in a preheated oven at 180°C (350°F) Gas 4 for 35-40 minutes, until the peaches are soft and tender, but still retain their shape, and the liquid has become syrupy. Remove from the oven and let cool slightly. Serve warm with the champagne syrup spooned over and lashings of whipped cream. Alternatively, cover and chill overnight for the flavours to fully develop. Remove the chilled peaches from the refrigerator and let stand at room temperature for about 20 mintures before serving with the syrup and whipped cream.

champagne sabayon

The French version of the Italian classic Zabaglione, made with fizz instead of marsala. Spoon into tall glasses and serve with wafer-thin biscuits, or serve poured over lightly poached fruit such as apricots, cherries, peaches or nectarines.

6 egg yolks
200 g caster sugar
¼ bottle brut fizz, such as Freixenet Cordón Negro NV
Serves 6

Put the egg yolks and sugar in a medium-sized mixing bowl and using a balloon whisk or electric hand-held beater, whisk vigorously until thick and creamy. Bring a saucepan of water to the boil, reduce the heat to barely simmering, then set the bowl over the pan. Check the water level – the bowl and water must not touch. Drizzle in the fizz as you whisk and continue whisking for about 15 minutes until the mixture is thick, fluffy and doubled in volume. Remove from the heat and serve immediately.

poached apricots

Apricots, peaches, nectarines and cherries – when in season – are ideal for poaching in a light sugar syrup. Choose one of these or a combination to gently poach and serve hot or at room temperature with champagne sabayon.

Poaching syrup:
3 tablespoons sugar
300 ml water

500 g apricots, peaches or nectarines, halved and stones
   removed, or cherries, left whole
Serves 6

In a small saucepan, dissolve the sugar in the water over low heat. Let boil for about 5 minutes until light and syrupy, then reduce the heat and add the fruit. Cook for about 10 minutes until the fruit is soft but still holds its shape. Transfer the poached fruit and syrup to a serving bowl. Serve hot or let cool, then serve.

champagne truffles

Velvety smooth chocolates that melt in the mouth are a perfect after-dinner treat with a cup of fine coffee. It is important to use a good-quality plain chocolate containing about 70 per cent cocoa solids. White chocolate will also make excellent truffles. Vary the coating if you wish and roll the champagne ganache in finely chopped nuts, icing sugar or dip in melted chocolate.

Champagne ganache:

275 g plain chocolate or white chocolate, finely chopped

175 ml double cream

25 g unsalted butter, softened

3-4 tablespoons Champagne, such as Lanson Black Label Brut NV

Coating, choose from:

good-quality, unsweetened cocoa powder

icing sugar

pistachio nuts, finely chopped

plain chocolate or white chocolate, melted

Makes about 20–30 truffles

To make the ganache, melt the chocolate in a bowl set over a saucepan of hot (not simmering water). Pour the cream into a small saucepan and bring it to the boil. Remove from the heat and pour the hot cream onto the melted chocolate. Using a wooden spoon, stir until thoroughly mixed, then add the softened butter and Champagne. Stir well to form a lump-free mixture. Let cool, then cover and chill in the refrigerator overnight.

Using two teaspoons, form the chilled ganache into 20-30 balls and as they are shaped, put onto a baking sheet lined with greaseproof paper. Chill the mixture if it becomes too soft to shape.

To coat, put the cocoa, icing sugar or chopped nuts in a bowl. Drop in the truffles, one at a time and roll to coat. If coating with melted chocolate, freeze the truffle balls for 1 hour then dip each one into the chocolate and coat well. Remove and let dry on a wire rack. Eat immediately or chill for up to 10 days.

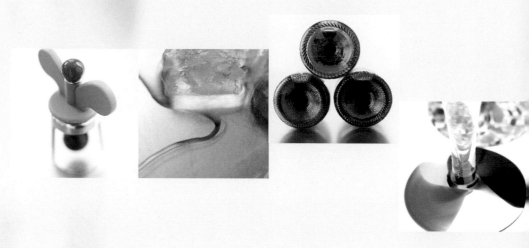

enjoying fizz

serving fizz

storing fizz

Fizz is a delicate and sensitive wine which will spoil if it is poorly stored. If you are going to keep fizz for more than two months it is best to store it in total darkness, undisturbed and at a constant temperature. Non-vintage Champagne benefits from six to eight months of storage – it tastes richer and more creamy. Always keep the bottles lying on their side, so that the cork stays wet at all times, otherwise it will dry out and shrink. Don't worry if you haven't got a cellar for short-term storage; under the bed in the spare room where the heating is turned off, or in a cupboard that is seldom opened will be fine. What is important is maintaining a steady temperature with little fluctuation. For long-term storage of one year or more, a cellar or basement is essential.

chilling fizz

Fizz always tastes best well chilled, but the exact temperature for chilling is a matter of personal taste. Three to four hours in the refrigerator is fine, or if you are caught unprepared, a 30-minute blast in the freezer will do the trick. A word of cautionary advice; don't forget about the bottle in the freezer – if the fizz freezes, the cork will shoot out and quite possibly the bottle will explode – I know, I've done it! If you are using an ice bucket to chill fizz, ice mixed with water will cool the fizz much faster than ice alone. Chilling fizz helps reduce the pressure inside the bottle so that it is easier and safer to open, and there is no wastage.

opening the bottle

To open a bottle correctly, take the foil off the top of the bottle, then place the thumb of your left hand on top of the cork and gently untwist the wire cage with your right hand. You can remove this completely, or leave it on. Point the bottle away from your body. Grasp the cork with the palm of your left hand, hold the bottle in your right hand and gently twist the bottle while holding the cork still. As long as the bottle has not been shaken, the cork should come out quite easily with a gentle pop and a line of smoke-like haze escaping from the bottle. It's a good idea to have a Champagne flute or saucer glass at the ready, so that you can capture those all-important bubbles if any do escape.

I experienced a far more dramatic way of opening a bottle of Champagne while visiting Canard-Duchêne at Rilly-La-Montagne. I was given a very large sword and shown how, if you tap (quite hard) the neck of the bottle, just below the cork in exactly the right place and with just the right amount of force, you can open the wine by making a clean break through the glass. I was amazed when I managed to open the bottle successfully in this fashion, and to this day I still cherish the glass top, cork and wire intact.

pouring fizz

If you are only serving a few glasses of fizz, it is easiest to tilt the glass first, as you would when pouring beer, so that when you pour it, the glass doesn't overflow with froth. But if you are pouring fizz for a big party, it is best to first pour a little fizz into each glass, to fill by one-third; then as soon as the froth has died down, top up the glasses. If it looks as if the foam will shoot over the top of the glass, quickly put your finger in the middle of the foam or dip the end of a teaspoon handle in the middle.

Jacquart 2000, 90, 94
Jacquart 1998 Cuvée Mosaïque, 95
Jacquart Brut Mosaïque NV, 45, 52
Jacquart Rosé 2000, 84, 94
Jacquesson, Avize Grand Cru 1996, 90, 95
Jacquesson Grand Vin Signature 1995, 95
jereboam, 138
Jordan, 11
Joseph Perrier 1998, 86
Joseph Perrier Cuvée Josephine 1995, 84
Joseph Perrier 1990 Cuvée Royale, 84, 94
Joseph Perrier Blanc de Blancs Brut NV, 76, 78
Joseph Perrier Cuvée Royale NV, 47, 52
Julep, Champagne, 109

Kir Royale, 11, 51, 63, 109
Korbel Blanc de Noirs NV, 75, 79
Korbel Brut NV, 31, 34, 42, 47, 52
Korbel Brut Rosé NV, 47, 53
Korbel Chardonnay NV, 10, 75, 79
Korbel Rouge NV, 104
Kornell Rouge NV, 104
Krone Borealis Brut NV, Cap Classique, 63, 67
Krug Clos du Mésnil 1979, 81, 86, 94
Krug Clos du Mésnil 1995, 86, 95
Krug Grande Cuvée NV, 7, 8, 69, 71, 72, 78
Krug Rosé NV, 63, 66
Krug Vintage 1990, 85, 95

Languedoc, 24
Langlois Crémant de Loire, 61, 66
Lanson 1961, 95
Lanson Noble Cuvée 1997, 95
Lanson Black Label Brut NV, 56, 61, 66, 124
Laurent-Perrier 1996, 84
Laurent-Perrier NV, 65, 66
lemon juice:
    Champagne St. Clements, 110
    Mexican Sunrise, 111
lime juice:
    Citrus Toast, 115
Limoux, 24
Lindauer Brut NV, 56, 63, 67, 116
Lindauer Brut Rosé NV, 44, 47, 53, 63
Lindauer Special Reserve NV, 35, 37, 53, 63
Loire Valley, 23, 45, 52, 61, 102
London, 8, 17
Louis Roederer, 17, 23, 85
Louis Roederer Brut Premier NV, 72, 78
Louis Roederer Brut Rosé NV, 47, 52
Louis Roederer Brut Vintage 1999, 85, 94
Louis Roederer Riche NV, 98, 102, 121
Louis Roederer Rosé 1999, 90, 94

Lumley, Joanna, 71
lunch, 35, 61, 75–6

Macabeo grape, 24
magnum, 55, 138
Marc Brédif Brut Vouvray, 45, 52
Marie Antoinette, Queen of France, 135
Marlborough, 26
Marlborough Deutz, 26
Mauzac grape, 24
medium-bodied fizz, 31–53
Melon Bubble, 114
Mendocino County, 25
Mercier, 23
Mercier NV, 61, 66
Méthode Cap Classique, 26
méthode champenoise, 19, 20
méthode traditionelle, 19, 20
methusalem, 138
Mexican Sunrise, 111
Midori:
    Melon Bubble, 114
mint:
    Champagne Julep, 109
Mitchell's, 104
Moët & Chandon, 17, 23, 25, 44, 75
Moët & Chandon 1999, 94
Moët & Chandon NV, 51, 52
Moët & Chandon Dom Pérignon, 81
Moët & Chandon Dom Pérignon 1998, 90, 95
Moët & Chandon Rosé 1999, 84, 94
Montana, 26
La Morandina, 103
Moscato d'Asti, 24, 58, 103, 108
Moscato grape, 24
mousse, 136
Müller-Thurgau grape, 26
Mumm, 25, 26
Mumm Cordon Rouge 1995, 88, 95
Mumm Cordon Rouge NV, 42, 52
Mumm de Cramant Grand Cru NV, 35, 45, 52
Mumm Cuvée Napa NV, 108, 116, 118
Mumm Napa Valley Blanc de Blancs NV, 75–6, 79
Mumm Sparkling Pinot Noir NV, 104
Muscat grape, 20, 24
mushrooms:
    Wild Mushroom and Champagne Risotto, 118

Nautilus Marlborough Cuvée NV, 72, 76, 79
nebuchadnezzar, 138
Negri, Marco, 58, 103
New Year's Eve, 85
New York State, 25

New Zealand, 8, 17, 26, 116
    aperitif-style fizz, 67
    full-bodied fizz, 79
    medium-bodied fizz, 53
Nicolas Feuillatte 1999, 90
Nicolas Feuillatte 2000, 94
Nicolas Feuillatte Grand Cru 1996, 90, 95
non-vintage (NV), 20
North America, 17, 24–5
    see also California
Nyetimber Blanc de Blancs 1995, 65

opening bottles, 129–30
orange juice:
    Buck's Fizz, 109
    Caribbean Cruiser, 113
    Citrus Toast, 115
    Texas Fizz, 113
outdoor meals, 42–4, 65

Pacific Northwest, 25
Parellada grape, 24
parties, 41–2, 61
peaches:
    Bellini, 109
    Bubbly Baked Peaches, 121
Penedés, 24
Peppertree Sparkling Shiraz NV, 104
Pérignon, Dom, 17
Pernod:
    Death In The Afternoon, 111
Perrier-Jouët, 17
Perrier-Jouët 1996 Cuvée Belle Epoque, 84, 95
Perrier-Jouët 1999 Cuvée Belle Epoque Rosé, 94
Perrier-Jouët NV, 34, 52
Pick-Me-Up, Champagne, 110
picnics, 44–7
Piedmont, 24
Pierre Jourdan Cuvée Belle Rose NV, 37
pincers, 133
pink fizz see rosés
Pinot Blanc grape, 23, 25
Pinot Meunier grape, 20, 21, 22
Pinot Noir grape, 20, 21, 22, 25, 26, 104
Piper Heidsieck, 10
Piper Heidsieck, 1996, 95
Piper Heidsieck Demi-Sec NV, 101, 102, 120
Piper Heidsieck NV, 52, 120
Piper Heidsieck Rosé NV, 65, 66
Poire William:
    Melon Bubble, 114
Pol Roger, 8, 87

Pol Roger Cuvée Sir Winston Churchill 1995, 85, 95
Pol Roger Demi-Sec NV, 98, 102
Pol Roger Rosé 1998, 87, 94
Pol Roger Sir Winston Churchill, 81
Pol Roger Vintage Brut 1998, 88, 95
Pol Roger White Foil NV, 56–7, 58, 63, 66
pouring fizz, 130
Prawns, Champagne, 116
prestige cuvées, 21, 69
puddings, sweet fizz to serve with, 98–101

quarter bottle, 138

R. de Ruinart Brut NV, 63, 66
Raimat Grand Brut NV, 71–2, 76, 79
recipes, 116–25
red fizz, 104–5
regions, 22–6
rehoboam, 138
remuage, 17, 19
restaurants, 56
riche fizz, 97
Risotto, Wild Mushroom and Champagne, 118
romantic occasions, 35–7, 58–61, 84
Rondel Premier Cuvée Brut NV, 61, 67
Rondel Premier Cuvée Demi-Sec NV, 101, 102
Rose-Petal and Champagne Sorbet, 120
rosés, 19
    aperitif–style fizz, 66, 67
    full–bodied fizz, 69, 78, 79
    medium–bodied fizz, 52, 53
    vintage Champagne, 94
rum:
    Calypso Fizz, 111
    Caribbean Cruiser, 113

Sabayon, Champagne, 123
St. Clements, Champagne, 110
St. Laurent, Yves, 23
Saki, 98
salmanazar, 138
Sandora Blanc de Blancs Cava Brut NV, 61, 67
Saracco Paolo, 103
saucer glasses, 135
Saumur, 23, 61
savoury dishes, demi–sec fizz to serve with, 101
Schramsberg Blanc de Noirs, 25
Schramsberg Napa Valley Crémant 1995, 101, 103
Schug Rouge de Noir 1996, 104
Seaview, 25, 116

Seaview Brut NV, 41, 47, 53
Seaview Brut Rosé NV, 8, 67
second fermentation, 19, 20
sediment, removing, 19
Seppelt, 25
Seppelt Great Western Brut Rosé NV, 61, 67
Seppelt Salinger 1992, 86, 95
Seppelt Sparkling Shiraz 1994, 104
serving fizz, 128–31
Shaw, George Bernard, 63
Shiraz grape, 20, 25, 104
Simon, André, 43
Sonoma County, 25
Sorbet, Champagne and Rose-Petal, 120
South Africa, 8, 26
    aperitif–style fizz, 67
    medium–bodied fizz, 53
Spain, 8, 17, 24
    aperitif–style fizz, 67
    demi–sec fizz, 102
    full–bodied fizz, 79
    medium–bodied fizz, 53
La Spinetta, 103
storing fizz, 129
stout:
    Black Velvet, 110
Strauss, Johann, 35
styles, 20–1
Sunday lunch, 61
supper, 47, 61–3
sweet fizz, 97–103
swizzle sticks, 133

Taittinger, 23, 25, 35, 86, 90
Taittinger 1999, 94
Taittinger Comtes de Champagnes Blanc de Blancs 1996, 95
Taittinger Comtes de Champagnes Rosé 1999, 86
Taittinger Prestige Rosé NV, 77, 78
tank method, 19
taste notes:
    aperitif–style fizz, 66–7
    demi–sec fizz, 102–3
    full–bodied fizz, 78–9
    medium–bodied fizz, 52–3
    red fizz 104
    vintage Champagne, 94–5
tequila:
    Mexican Sunrise, 111
terminology, 20–1
Texas Fizz, 113
Thackeray, W.M., 88
Tovey, Charles, 60
Truffles, Champagne, 124

ultra brut, 21
United Kingdom see England
United States of America, 24–5
    aperitif–style fizz, 66–7
    demi–sec fizz, 103
    full–bodied fizz, 79
    medium–bodied fizz, 52–3
    red fizz, 104

vermouth:
    Champagne Pick-Me-Up, 110
Veuve Clicquot La Grande Dame 1996, 11, 81, 90, 95
Veuve Clicquot La Grande Dame Rosé 1995, 87, 94
Veuve Clicquot Ponsardin, 17
Veuve Clicquot Rosé 1999, 87, 94
Veuve Clicquot Vintage Réserve 1990, 87, 94
Veuve Clicquot Rich 1999, 87, 94
Veuve Clicquot Yellow Label NV, 42, 52
Victoria, 25
Vignaioli di Santo Stefano Belbo, 103
vintage fizz, 21, 81–95
vodka:
    Cherry Froth, 113
Vouvray, 23, 45, 51

Washington State, 25
Waugh, Evelyn, 38–9
weddings, 51, 65, 75, 86–7
winemaking, 19
wire muzzles, 19

Xarel–lo grape, 24

Yaldara Reserve Brut NV, 53, 61–3, 67
Yaldara Reserve Brut Rosé NV, 56, 67
Yalumba Cuvée One Pinot Noir Chardonnay NV, 42, 51, 53
Yalumba Cuvée Two Sparkling Cabernet NV, 104
Yarra Valley, 25
yeast, 19

acknowledgements

Picture Credits
p.14 *left and centre left inset* Mick Rock, Cephas; **p.16** *top left* courtesy of Bollinger; **p.16** *below left* Hulton Getty, *right* taken from a poster by Jean de'Ylen published in 1921 – courtesy of Joseph-Perrier; **p.17** courtesy of Mumm; **p.20** *right* Maurice Huser, Tony Stone Images; **pp.20-21** Michael Busselle, Tony Stone Images; **p.20** *left and left centre inset* Mick Rock, Cephas.

With thanks to Belinda and Guy Battle and everyone else who allowed us to photograph in their homes.

Acknowledgements
My grateful thanks to members of the wine trade who supplied bottles of Champagne and sparkling wine as well as information for this book. Special thanks are due to Vicky Bishop, Fiona Campbell, Susie Harris, Gilly Mackwood and from the California Wine Institute, John MacLaren. I would also like to thank my father, Dominic King, for the loan of his beautiful Georgian glasses and my agent Caryl Skelton. Thanks also to Peter Cassidy, who made the images come alive through his sensational photographs that far surpassed anything I could have imagined. A big thank you to all the team at Ryland Peters & Small for their hard work in putting this book together so beautifully, and especially to Anne Ryland who gave me the opportunity to write *Fabulous Fizz* and Louise Leffler who designed such a wonderful book. And last but not least, thanks to Sally Lester who typed the manuscript and without whom this book could not have been written.

The publishers and author would like to thank all the Champagne houses who so generously gave bottles of fizz for photography and to the following companies who loaned the glassware, cutlery, crockery, table linen and accessories that appear in the book:

Asprey & Garrard
167 New Bond Street
London W1
www.asprey-garrard.com

The Conran Shop Chelsea
Michelin House
81 Fulham Road
London SW3
020 7589 7401
www.conran.co.uk

EGG
36 Kinnerton Street
London SW1
020 7235 9315

Nicole Farhi Homestore
www.nicolefarhi.com

Thomas Goode
19 South Audley Street
London W1
020 7499 2823

Heal's
196 Tottenham Court Road
London W1
020 7636 1666
www.heals.co.uk

Michael Johnson Ceramics
81 Kingsgate Road
London NW6
020 7624 2493
UK distributors for Reidel glasses

Ruffle & Hook
122 St John's Street
London EC1
020 7490 4321